We Laughed... We Cried...
...We Ate Dog Biscuits!

By MaryLee Marilee

Based on Humor/Life Style Newspaper Columns
of MaryLee Marilee

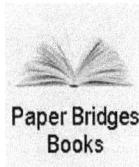

Paper Bridges
Books

Published by Paper Bridges
December, 2013

Disclaimer:

This is a work taken from the Newspaper Columns: *Confessions of a Crackpot, Rolling Along,* and *The Crackpot,* by MaryLee Marilee, published by Graphic Publications in three to five weekly newspapers from 1994 - 2006. All names, characters, places and incidents used by the author are attribute-able to her, and to her alone. Any references to actual people, living, dead (or otherwise incarnate), or to events or locales is entirely coincidental.

If you think you recognize someone within these pages, all I can say (as my old, writing professor used to say) is that "it's all grist for the mill!"

To my family, I ask their forgiveness for exposing them to any undue stress as a result of reporting life as it happens: *that's the breaks, when you have a writer in the family!*

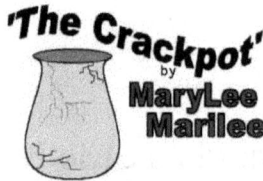

'The Crackpot'
by
MaryLee Marilee

Book Copyright © 2013 by MaryLee Marilee

Book design by MaryLee Marilee

Cover & author photos by Gwyneth Hollenbach
Photo credit to Suzanne Conrad

ISBN: 978-0-9831765-7-2   Print Book

ISBN: 978-0-9831765-6-5   E-Book

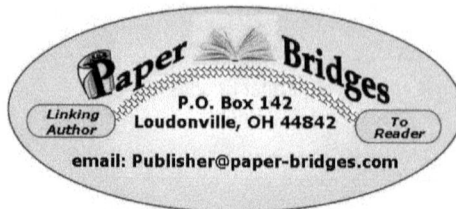

Paper Bridges

Linking Author

P.O. Box 142
Loudonville, OH 44842

To Reader

email: Publisher@paper-bridges.com

ALSO BY THE AUTHOR:

The Hearthstones Series
(Historical Fiction)
(MaryLee Marilee with Sheryl Drake Lawrence)

Book I
Keep the Home Fires Burning

Book II
Let the Sparks Fly!

Book III
Glowing Embers

(Available at Amazon.com and BarnesandNoble.com)

Contents:

We Ate Dog Biscuits

<u>Dedication</u>

For Dr. Jay D. Haar, without whom my earthly journey would have been much shorter, and a whole lot less productive.

Thanks, Dr. Haar!

Introduction

Humor

"If you want to tell people the truth, you had better make them laugh, or they'll kill you." George B. Shaw

"Is there money in farming?" asks a young man to a farmer.

"Sure, there's money in farming," he answers.

"How much is there?"

"Lots of it. I know, cause I left all mine there."

Humor—it's the grease that makes cutting truths slippery enough to swallow.

But a sense of humor is a nebulous sort of thing, because not everyone sees this crazy world of ours in quite the same light as does his neighbor.

The banana-peel slip that makes one person laugh, makes another shake his head in disdain. Or the off-color joke that cracks up all the guys at deer camp will most likely offend the ladies at the quilting society.

What may, in fact, appear funny to one person, can cause serious offense to another.

Makes telling a joke in some circles quite a challenge. Of course, if you're like me and can never remember the punch line, it's no big sacrifice to avoid the joke-telling altogether.

However, in order to survive in this hectic culture of ours, it's essential to possess a good sense of humor. Mental and emotional health depend on the ability to laugh at ourselves.

I have a plaque that says, *"Life is easier than you think. All you have to do is accept the impossible, do without the indispensable, and be able to smile at anything."*

When you lose your job, have a mountain of bills to pay, and the phone keeps ringing with collectors looking for payment, you could get really upset and become downright grouchy with those callers (who are just doing their jobs, by the way. And I'd bet my lottery ticket, they're having no picnic calling you, either).

Instead you could reach deep into your humor reserves and look at the situation in a completely different light, in order to carry on a civil conversation in such an emotionally charged context:

> *"You say I need to send how much before you shut off my electricity? Hey, I put all this month's bills into the basket, and I can only pick out five of them to pay with the money I made from selling my oldest child. If you keep bugging me like this, next month when I sell my youngest, I won't even put your bill in the basket!*
>
> *"But seriously, I need your help, here. How can we figure out a creative way to work this out?"*

By calling upon a bit of humor, we can learn to diffuse the stickiest of situations and turn a negative encounter into one that can have positive results. And by asking ourselves, "What's the worst thing that could happen here, anyway?" we can more easily accept a less-than-perfect situation with aplomb.

So, they turn off the electricity—which means the kids can no longer watch TV, we learn to interact as a family by kerosene light over the Monopoly board, and we actually communicate with one another. (That's really so terrible?)

Why not contribute less to the buy-buy-buy mentality of a materialistic world and learn to improvise and make do with what we already have?

Inevitably, you will face a situation when you can no longer laugh. When that happens to you, don't wait—*SEEK HELP IMMEDIATELY*. Without laughter, life holds little enough in the way of pleasure. Fortunately, we live in a time that's rich in resources to help us cope.

Next time you face a crisis, look deep into the situation and find something about it that can make you laugh—or at the very least, smile.

For when we learn to laugh at ourselves and not take things so seriously, only then can we finally appreciate this roller-coaster ride called life and begin to digest its truths—cuz it takes a healthy dose of humor to choke down some of them.

I present the offerings in this book, with the hope that you can find a few kernels of truth, while laughing them down with a bit of humor.

"We Laughed... (pretty self explanatory)

...We Cried... (cleansing therapy for the soul)

...We Ate Dog Biscuits! (crazy escapades bringing both!)

Happy Reading!

We Laughed...

Good, Clean Country Air

Take a whiff. What does it smell like to you here?

Evidently one visitor to Amish county has a "strong" opinion, judging from a recent letter that came to the *Graphic Publications'* editorial department via fax.

I can't help myself, I simply have to respond. But first, a portion of that letter:

> *"...I realize that the area is a large, rural farming community, but more has to be done on the manure odor that we have to deal with every time we visit.... it's your responsibility to make sure that these farms are clean, which I feel you are not doing enough about...*

> *"Can you make out an agreement with the farmers on ways of dealing with the manure and livestock odor, such as chemicals or sprays. Another problem which annoys me, is look at any typical pasture field, and you will see lumps of manure, which should be cleaned up and used for fertilizer... the lumps which fall onto the road should also be cleaned up by county engineers because it looks filthy and can spread disease."*

Now as a dyed-in-the-wool country girl, I've shoveled my share over the years. (Mind you, I'm not talking barnyard dung only here.) I have to admit, at times the smell of the literal stuff *can* overwhelm those not accustomed to it.

I prefer the smell of sheep or horse manure, myself. Now that I'm acquainted with llamas, their scent falls in that category, too. Steer manure I can tolerate, but dairy waste has a distinct rotten-silage-sour-milk aroma that tends to make me a little nauseous.

The hog smell poses a different problem altogether. You see, Daddy always told us that odor "smelled like money" to him.

It just made me sneeze like crazy.

> *... one man's odor is another man's perfume!*

That leaves only chickens, and I hesitate to even comment on the whole poultry end of things, except to say chicken that manure grows the best tomatoes and strawberries you'll ever hope to find.

My daughter always tried to run down any wandering chickens whenever she'd drive in our lane. I tend to share her opinion of poultry—definitely some of the most brainless animals God ever created.

You can see the problem with farm odors: the ones we get used to, we seldom notice at all, but to visitors unfamiliar with them, they can definitely cause offense.

But, let's turn the tables a moment; how does a country nose react in the city?

When we "country kids" would go to visit our city grandma, the factory stench and auto exhaust fumes offended us far more than the aroma of our own "good, clean, country air." We'd tease each other and say we had to go back home just to "blow the stink off."

So you see, it all boils down to a matter of perspective, no?

I always figured that in order to understand those who are different from us, we needed to examine the differences with an open mind, not try to change them into something more aesthetically pleasing to our own tastes.

After all, one man's odor is another man's perfume!

Even a skunk will tell you that!

Space Cadet strikes again!

Ever have one of *those* days when your brain doesn't quite kick in? When pulling your head back under the covers looks like the best choice you could possibly make?

You know the kind I mean. It all starts out innocently enough, but as soon as you swing one foot over the edge of the bed, things just begin to "happen to you."

You trip over your slippers, you spit out toothpaste and miss the sink, and in the process of making your morning "cup-o-Joe" you spill coffee grounds all over the floor. To top that off, when the coffee maker starts to perk away, you discover you forgot to put the pot underneath the basket and now you have coffee running all over the counter.

Welcome to one of *"those days."*

I woke up fuzzy-headed this morning and have proceeded to walk into walls all day long—figuratively and quite literally, I might add.

First off, I spent two hours working on the computer, only to have my entire document disappear into never-never land before I remembered to hit the "save" command. (You'd think a body who spends the greater part of her day writing would have learned that by now, wouldn't you?)

Not to worry. I can always switch to sewing when the writing gets too frustrating.

But today, before I could even begin working on my current bridal project, I spent one entire hour hunting for my sewing scissors, only to discover that they lay in plain sight, right on top of my sewing machine all along. (I swear they weren't there when I looked before.)

O.K., I could finally start sewing. But guess what I did straight off? You guessed it—I sewed the bodice of this dress on backwards. Time to get out the seam ripper. (Now, where in

3

blazes did I put that blasted seam ripper? Wasn't it right here just a minute ago?)

"Bernie," my Bernina sewing machine, has also decided that today would be a good day to give me grief. Naturally, I have four dresses to get ready for bridal fittings. O.K., maybe after a little rest Bernie will decide to work properly again.

I'll just take time out to feed the dogs. Since I always like to mix in a little something to make that dry dog food go down easier—and since I had just cooked some bacon the day before—I put the frying pan back on the stove to liquefy the hardened bacon fat, so I could stir a little bit into their food.

I had INTENDED to leave that pan on the burner for only a minute, mind you, but the phone rang.

You can guess what happened next.

SMOKE ALARM!

I grabbed the cast-iron pan's hot handle with a dish towel (I may have been spacey, but I'm not stupid), and I carried the pot outside onto the deck, where the smoke could dissipate. However, in the strong wind, one corner of that dish towel ended up flopping over, right into that pan. Soooooooo, now I had one grease-soaked towel to deal with.

Time for another load of laundry. First, I needed to take the last load out of the washer and put it out to dry. I opened up the washing machine.

Nothing.

Can you believe it? I ran that last, entire wash cycle without putting any clothes in there!

Maybe I should just go back to bed and start this morning all over again.

Raise your voice and stretch your soul

"Laa Laaaa, la la Laa, la la Laa, la la LAAAAAAA . . . "

"Excuse me, ma'am," says the woman sitting next to me, "but you're supposed to be singing the words."

"Oh, you mean these garbled letters underneath all those little black things?"

"Those are called notes, dear."

"Yes, of course. I really can read music, you know. But I must admit, I'm having trouble recognizing any of these words."

"That's because they're Italian. All the best operas are written in Italian, you know."

"No. I didn't."

"Well, now you do, dear. And if it wouldn't trouble you too much, I think you should try to sing the words as well as the notes," says my musical compatriot, refocusing on her own score.

In case you're wondering about all this singing business, perhaps I'd better explain. You see, a few weeks ago I noticed a small notice in my newspaper which announced that the Mansfield Symphony Choir would be holding open auditions for potential chorus members.

Being of an optimistic bent, and reasonable talent, I decided to give it a try. Hey, the worst they could tell me was, "Sorry ma'am, but we don't need any voices *quite* like yours." (If this writing business has done nothing else, it has helped steel me for rejection.)

I proceeded to prepare my try-out selection.

I think I should mention here, that although I have done some solo work in the past, my entire musical repertoire of late has

> You know the old saying, *"Music calms the savage beast"... music can also rebuild the shattered soul.*

encompassed solitary concerts given in the grand amphitheater of stately pines located deep in the Mohican Memorial State Forest, which adjoins our property.

If a body can't let loose and SING out there, where can she? No one but deer, 'coon and coyotes to object.

"I sing because I'm happyyyy, I sing because I'm FREEE . . ."

I ask you, what self-respecting varmint could possibly object to those lyrics? To the caterwauling, maybe, but to the words— never!

Besides, they're getting used to this Crackpot invading their tranquil haven and periodically exploding into song.

If tripping down this rocky life's-path has taught me nothing else, I have learned that in order to stay healthy and relatively sane, I need to release *all* my pent-up emotions. Otherwise, this "pot" is apt to "crack" once more.

What better way to do that, than in song?

You know the old saying, "Music calms the savage beast." I'd like to amend that statement and also say that "music can rebuild the shattered soul."

Well, you already know the rest of the story: I tried out for the Symphony Chorus, and wonder of wonders, I made it! The conductor did say that although he liked the quality of my voice, I did sound a bit "rusty." (Good thing I have a daughter who gives voice lessons!)

Last week I attended my first rehearsal and had the opportunity to peruse music for the first concert in which I'll participate: "Operas' Greatest Hits"— to be sung in Italian.

Gulp! I think I'm in WAY over my head, here. Well what the hey! I've never been one to shrink from the challenge of s-t-r-e-t-c-h-i-n-g myself a bit.

"Leee bee-aam, amor fraaa, aah aah aah ka leee cheeee peew kal deee ba chee eee aaah vra!"

I feel the strategically placed poke of a pointy elbow.

6

"Spare me, please, dear! Perhaps you *should* just stick to 'La la las' for now," says my chorale cohort.

Far be it from me not to comply with another's request.

"Laa Laaaa, la la Laa, la la Laa, la la LAAAAAAA . . . "

Forgive me, Giuseppe Verdi. (In case you can't translate Italian, that's Joe Green to you!)

I do promise to do better by performance time.

Right way, wrong way. Which way, you say?

Before I go into my little "adventure" of late, let me just say that Mansfield is FULL of one-way streets, which, after 30+ years of driving around in that city, STILL confound me. (I guess some of us are just slow learners.)

Well after Symphony Choir practice in Mansfield recently, I got another crack at "getting it right." For you see, the maestro had changed the location of our choir-practice site to Richland Academy for the Arts, located smack dab in downtown Mansfield.

Nice building, on (you guessed it) one way streets, as are all the parking lots in that well-lighted neighborhood. I gave myself plenty of time before practice to FIND the right place, then to find a PARKING spot—and I managed to maneuver down all the one-ways just fine.

Wheew!

By the time practice ended nearly three hours later (around 10 p.m.), it was dark, windy, and rather warm. The streets were pretty well devoid of traffic and the parking lot mostly empty, except for a police cruiser sitting over at the side. (Mansfield Police Station is located one block away from that parking lot).

I got in my trusty little red truck, got myself all settled—seat belt fastened, back pillow adjusted—then started up the engine and took off. I made my exit from the parking lot the same way I had entered, heading south toward home.

Only one problem: that was a one-way street heading north. *Ooooops!*

But I had fully turned before I realized my mistake, so at the first intersection I turned right to catch the parallel street on the next block heading south.

So far, so good, no traffic at least.

HOWEVER, after I'd made the next turn onto the correct, one-way street heading south, I saw the flashing gumball-lights of aforementioned police car pulling up behind me.

8

Drats!

O.K., so I pulled over, whereupon I discovered that I had also forgotten to turn on my headlights!

Double drats! (Did I mention that section of town had LOTS of lights, so who knew?)

"Excuse me, Ma'am," asked the young police officer shining his light into my eyes, "but do you know why I stopped you?"

"One way street, wrong way. Right? I get turned around every time I drive in this crazy town! Say, you don't have any GOOD maps of this city with the one-way streets CLEARLY marked, do you?"

"Nope," says he. "What else?"

"I forgot to turn on my lights."

"Bingo. All right, I need your driver's license, vehicle registration and proof of insurance, please."

So, I proceed to dig for all the necessary documentation.

Then I wait. And I wait. And I wait some more.

I could just imagine the conversation going on back in that cruiser between the officers and central dispatch: "Last name, Marilee; first name, MaryLee... O.K. what gives? Are you guys trying to be funny here?", "No, dispatch, that's really the name on this license and registration. First name MaryLee with a 'y,' last name Marilee with an 'i.' That's the truth!"

By the time the officers (two of 'em now, the original young man and a younger-looking woman) returned to my driver's side window, I had my purse cleaned out, the glove box reorganized and several new radio stations picked out.

"We're just finding all kinds of things with you, tonight, Ma'am," says the lady officer with a smile. "You're current as far as your registration goes, but you have an expired sticker on your license plate. Do you know what happened to this year's sticker?"

I didn't have to play dumb, because I WAS dumb! ... I screwed up, pure and simple.

(Ooo boy, just what I need.) "I'm certain that I put that thing on there by my last birthday," I tell them with true conviction. "I can't imagine what could have happened to it."

"They make the glue on those stickers tamper-proof, you know. They can't just fall off. And if anyone tried to pull or scrape it off, it'd be quite evident."

"Well, can I get a replacement sticker?" I ask the officer.

"You'll have to take that up with the Bureau of Motor Vehicles, Ma'am. Here are all your papers back," says he, handing me the fist-full of documents.

I nonchalantly shuffle through the papers, whereupon I find said orange sticker buried between the folds.

"Geeze, look what I just found! I could have SWORN I put that thing on there!"

"Well, we'll give you a written warning this time, Ma'am. But I think you'd better fasten that sticker on your license plate as soon as you get home. By the way, don't forget to turn your lights on."

"Hey, I live in the country where it's DARK. Believe me, it's quite evident when you forget to turn your lights on out there."

"Have a nice evening, Ma'am. And a CAREFUL one!"

Need I mention my RELIEF at receiving just a warning?

I must tell the truth here: my reaction to this whole incident surprised and encouraged me. No adrenaline rush, no panic—I felt calm, cool and quite confident throughout the entire interview.

I didn't try to talk my way out of anything, I didn't fuss and fume, I didn't have to play dumb (because I WAS dumb!) I just shook my head and smiled at the officers, answered their questions honestly, and accepted their remarks with aplomb.

I screwed up, pure and simple.

The result: nothing worse than a written warning. And I think I know why: no doubt about it—I supplied their comic relief for the evening!

Time for Klara Klutz dues!

Whoops! Eeeeeeyiiiiieeee!!

Give me a sky hook and hold me up, Hannah!

Oh good grief, not again. Ice packs and ankle brace, here I come.

I should have *known* something like this was coming. Once more, it's time to pay my annual dues to the "Klara Klutz Klub."

As an established member of aforementioned clumsy coalition I can verify that I have fulfilled my compulsory obligation to maintain membership in good standing for yet, another year.

You see, I don't seem to have the ability to remain upright on my feet. (Just ask my chiropractor if you think I jest.)

I thought after the last stupid fall I'd finally learned my lesson about bumbling along watching stars or snowflakes, instead of keeping my eyes glued to the ground in front.

Geeze, I've even trained myself to count steps as I descend a stairway, feeling for that last step even after I've hit terra firma at the bottom.

You'd think I'd have this falling-down-thing under control by now, wouldn't you?

But without people like me tripping through life, who'd keep Klara Klutz alive? Or the chiropractors in business?

My latest foot-work faux-pas happened as I stumbled down-stairs in the dark on my way to bed last evening. You've got to understand, that I'm a morning person. When 4 or 5 a.m. rolls around, I bounce up to start my day.

Of course, that means by 7 or 8 p.m., the brain fog rolls in, and I begin to wilt.

Dangerous territory, that.

By now I should *know* to stay extra alert when navigating steps in such a foggy condition.

> *Every upstanding Klara Klutz already has a complete dispensary at her disposal...*

But alas, last night, as I took what I THOUGHT was the final step down and lit out to walk away from the stairs, SNAP! Bang, *KABOOM*!

Sprained ankle, here we go again.

Naturally, it's the same one I injured last year when I so carelessly stepped off another set of stairs gazing at Orion, instead of watching where I planted my feet. That poor ankle had finally, *almost*, gotten back to normal, although it still looks a bit thicker than its left-sided partner.

Sooooooo, after my ungraceful landing, I crawled my way to the freezer to break out an ice pack, downed a giant-sized dose of anti-inflammatory Advil®, then spent the rest of the night attempting to sleep on the couch, as I did my best to keep the ice pack from sliding off my stiffening ankle.

Why didn't I go to the emergency room, you ask?

What for? To rouse the entire house and have everyone lose a night's sleep? To have the hospital charge me $500+ for crutches, X-rays and Ace® bandages, then tell me to go home and prop my foot up with ice?

Every upstanding—or rather down-falling—Klara Klutz Klub member already has a complete dispensary at her disposal, stocked with just such items, and more. Why go to the bother and expense of raising my insurance rates, yet again, when there's nothing further medical experts can do anyway?

Hey, I can still wiggle my toes, so I know the thing's not broken. And it bears weight well enough to gimp along. I'll just have to explain my stupidity every time I make my way into public view for a while, that's all.

So, break out the ankle brace and strap on the football padding, 'cuz once we belong to Klara Klutz, our membership is irevocable.

(Besides, Klara keeps us all humble—not to mention well stocked with prosthetic devices.)

The truth, the whole truth, and nothing but the truth...

"Do you solemnly swear, to tell the truth, the whole truth, and nothing but the truth, so help you God?"

"I do."

"Take the witness stand."

So commenced questioning in Municipal Court, where I recently fulfilled my civic obligation, after receiving notification to appear for jury duty.

When Lady Justice calls, every good citizen must do her part.

My part required that I report along with nearly 30 other people, from whom the State and the Accused would select a jury.

So be it.

Upon entering the building, first thing out of the box—a metal detector. The X-ray man greeted me with a smile and checked my name off his list.

Beep! Beep! Beep!

Drat. Set one off again.

Once verifying that I carried no guns, bombs or contraband on my person, he directed me to the appropriate courtroom for this day's legal contest.

Seated among the other potential jurors, we waited... and we waited. As with all things governmental, hurry-up-and-wait definitely applies.

At last, the bailiff emerged. "All rise."

His Honor entered the courtroom.

After receiving a nutshell synopsis of the case at hand, the judge called eight people forward to pre-appointed seats in the jury box.

Hallelujah! He missed me! But, I was not home free quite yet.

In case one of the pre-selected souls should be excused from serving, the rest of us had to remain.

No problem. Out of 20+ people, what's the chance they'd actually call me next?

Questioning began with the prosecution; the defense followed up with more inquiries of each juror. After 20 minutes of intense scowls and dramatic pauses, the defense attorney requested that the judge excuse one juror.

"Very well. You may step down. Next I call MaryLee Marilee." He looked at the bailiff. "Is that right?"

"That's me!" I popped up from my seat made my way forward.

This courtroom is laid out quite nicely, as courtrooms go. But in order to get into the jury box, one must open and close three, different, swinging gates.

"They sure don't make it easy to get up here, do they," I said, rounding the last corner and squeezing past jurors legs to reach the empty seat.

"Ms. Marilee," began the defense attorney. "Is that your real name?"

"Yes, that's really my name." As a result of all the chuckling, the atmosphere had lightened up considerably.

"Do you have responses to any of the questions asked so far?"

"Yes, I have served on a jury in the past; that experience was educational, to say the least."

"I see you're a writer. Have you had occasion to write about the justice or law-enforcement systems?"

"As a matter of fact, I happen to be the first woman who spent a night in the new, Holmes County Jail," I said with pride. Humming broke out around the room. "They needed guinea pigs during the shakedown... before they opened the jail up for business. I wrote about it for my newspaper, of course."

"Have you written about judges or lawyers?"

"Yes."

"Anything detrimental or offensive?"

> *When Lady Justice calls, every good citizen must do her part.*

"Just the facts, nothing but the facts," I said with a smile.

More giggling broke out around the room. This time, even the judge laughed.

"One last question, Your Honor," said the defense attorney, turning to me. "Given the definitions you've heard about holding the defendant not guilty until proof of guilt has been established, do you think you can proceed with an open mind?"

"If an open mind means the same thing as having a hole in your head, of course I can."

"Let me re-phrase the question. Would you want someone like you on a jury if *you* were the one sitting in that defendant's seat?"

"Of course!"

Let me hasten to say, I executed my duty with rapt attention to the evidence, and I participated in serious discussions with my peers, as we deliberated toward a just verdict.

However, in my humble opinion, Lady Justice could definitely use more comic relief in her courtrooms.

'Perks' of growing older

Pimple. Blemish. Blackhead. Zit.

Whatever you want to call them, you wouldn't think that a woman over 50 would have to worry about them, now, would you?

Pimples are supposedly the bane of teenage years, not middle age. So how come they decide to reappear en masse as I approach these so-called "matronly" years?

Who ever heard of an old lady with zits?

To be honest, I don't feel very matron-like. Although my mirror tells me otherwise, the person looking out from these eyes still feels 35 years old. (I used to say 27, but I've adjusted the inner clock forward a bit, now that I'm an official Grandma.)

Oh, I know this body's beginning to show some wear and tear. The ankle I sprained over a year ago appears much thicker than its counterpart, and it still likes to trip me up from time to time, which is one reason I've taken to wearing these knee-length, lace-up moccasins.

Several of my joints can now warn of approaching low-pressure fronts, and I have one knuckle that's particularly sensitive to impending thunderstorms.

I could also do a whole monologue about the aggravation of wearing glasses (these days my eyes need trifocal help to see things without fuzz), but Bill Cosby has already done that much better than any Crackpot ever could.

I have noticed one interesting phenomenon: when I first get up in the morning, I can see better than at any other time of the day. Sometimes I can even read the morning paper without glasses!

Course, I have to lay the paper out on the table and stand four or five feet away, but hey, you do whatever works, right? I look at those newspaper gymnastics as a sort of challenge that I need to set for myself every few days.

Now I do realize that certain "changes" occur within the female anatomy as it approaches this mid-life season. And with all the Baby-Boomers passing middle age, every other TV commercial would seem to address delicate issues of this sort.

Don't worry, I will remain within the bounds of good taste here and NOT recapitulate the mysterious and sundry details of such bodily shifts. The only reason I broach the subject now is because of these dog-gone zits!

I have discovered one definite benefit in this passage of ripening age: lunacy. At no other time of a woman's life is she given license to act a little daft. From time to time hormonal imbalances can cause strange behavior that's completely out of a person's control.

Hallelujah! At last I've landed in a stage of life where I finally feel at home!

If I sell my truck and take to riding a bicycle, no one really bats an eye, because "she's going through the change."

If I give up the comfort of a perfectly wonderful new house for the stoic confines of a tipi, people might raise an eyebrow, but, hey, it's O.K. because "she's going through the change!"

If I decide to row a canoe from the Mohican River all the way down to New Orleans, people will say, "You go, girl!" to my face, but will whisper behind a hand, "Don't worry, it's just a phase. You *know* she's going through the change."

But there's something you need to understand here: I believe it takes a certain amount of maturity to recognize the importance of being nuts enough to tackle the outrageous.

Such pursuits give birth to genius.

In a manner of speaking, I do feel a real kinship with the pimple-faced teens who stand on the brink of life, ready to dive into the big pool of adulthood and splash around a bit. I've done my share of splashing in here; I've swallowed my share of water and come up sputtering on more than one occasion. But now, rather than lie back and float around in this watery deep,

> *I believe it takes a certain amount of maturity to recognize the importance of being nuts enough to tackle the outrageous.*

I'm finally ready try some of those dives I was too chicken to attempt when I had to be "the responsible adult."

Remember this: if you don't want to grow old inside, you must keep trying new things—whether it's a double-gainer from the high board, or a pollywog jump into the nearest puddle.

When we fail to attempt new challenges, we begin to die inside. I've got news for you: old age has more to do with flimsy attitudes and outmoded ideas than it does with fallen arches or flabby thighs.

That, my dear friend, is the true gauge which measures one's youth or age: inner vitality.

(It also helps to have a few screws loose—just to keep things in perspective!)

O.K. It's time for me to climb up this high diving board and attempt a double-twist, triple-flip back dive—and hope to high heaven I don't break my neck trying!

(Don't worry, I do have a good insurance man.)

To everything there is a season…

"To everything, there is a season, and a time
for every purpose under heaven."

The season of Motherhood has definitely passed by this particular Crackpot of a Grandmother.

After spending the last week filling in as "Surrogate Mom" for my Tennessee crew, I can tell you this is one Grandma who's moved WAAAAAAY beyond her time of mothering.

Oh, all the instincts come back quickly enough: Don't ask why, just DO it!; Keep that stick away from your sister, you'll poke her eye out; When I call you, I expect you to *come*!

It's just that as the Grandma, I'd much rather be the one doing all the fun things at this stage of the game, rather than acting as the designated drill sergeant.

But when Mom's not around, SOMEONE has to keep the troops moving ahead, right? Of course right!

Now, I don't want to create the impression that this visit has encompassed nothing more than an endless round of enforcing rules and regulations and household chores (not to mention keeping up with the T-Ball schedule).

We've had our fun times, too.

Enter Daniel and Tessa's first, camping trip away from home in Grandma's camper.

We loaded up food, clothes and walking sticks (they can come in handy when you need a little positive, posterior reinforcement [not that I'd ever use them on my grandkids, mind you. Just the threat of such a happenstance gave the appropriate incentive to keep aforementioned rascals in line]), and we headed off to Roan Mountain State Park Campground for our overnight adventure.

The weather looked clear when we left, but the further up the mountain we traveled, the more cloudy it became. We arrived at the campground in the middle of a gully-washer of a downpour.

No problem. We set up camp in the rain next to a protected hillside (driving a little motor home does have advantages over pitching a tent), and waited for the weather to clear so we could register our site with the park ranger.

Meanwhile, I tried to come up with enough interesting, inside activities to keep a very active four- and six-year-old occupied.

Did I happen to mention that this Grandmother has a jar where she collects any marbles she happens to find lying around loose? On this trip, the jar lost a substantial number.

Too bad I couldn't put my hooligans to work hunting for them. But, of course, the particular kind of marbles to which I refer have no substance whatsoever.

Daniel and Tessa Rose did manage to have a great time on our little camp-out. Since this introduced a whole, new experience for them, they had no frame of reference against which to measure its failings.

We turned our rainy expedition into quite the adventure, and they even found new friends in the six children (ages 1-13) occupying the campsite adjacent to ours (talk about a woman in the thick of mothering years—and she home-schools them all, to boot. Hats off to her fortitude!)

Kids definitely have a way of keeping a body honest.

Our next adventure will entail finding our way to Tri-Cities Airport to meet Mommy and Daddy, as they return from their trip to Spokane, Washington.

Wish me luck. I have a handy-dandy map to find our way there, and two, terrific back-seat drivers to make sure I don't miss a single turn.

"Wait! Wait! Tessa doesn't have her belt fastened!"

"Don't forget to fasten YOUR seatbelt, Grandma."

"Slow down, Grandma! You're going too fast!"

Kids definitely have a way of keeping a body honest.

"Can I have a drink? I'm thirsty."

"Daniel took my game! I want my game back!"

"It's not your game, Tessa, it's MINE."

"How long till we get there?"

"Are we there yet?"

Tell me, tell me, P-L-E-A-S-E (says this marble-less Grandma) that Mommy and Daddy did NOT miss any of their connecting flights!

I send my deepest respect to gutsy grandmas in their autumn years who have taken on the responsibility of raising grandchildren.

The Crackpot Campaign Ribbon for duty "above and beyond" goes out to you!

Firebug

Nothing soothes body and soul quite like a campfire. And nothing else smells quite like a campfire, either.

Living in the center of the camping world, as I do here below Loudonville, on any given weekend, I get to enjoy the scent of a wood fire without expending the effort to build one. Most mornings a person can smell campfire smoke wafting through this whole Mohican valley. It's a nice way to start the day.

But there's something that feels almost sacred in the process of building your own fire—sort of puts you in touch with all those ancestors who ever laid wood to hearth.

Can you build a good fire? There's an art to it, you know—ask any Girl Scout worth her badges.

It just so happens, that during my Girl-Scout camping days (a few lifetimes ago, at least), I learned the rules for building the perfect campfire.

Rule number one: ALWAYS keep your matches dry.

Rule number two: You can't start a fire with two-inch logs, so make sure you have plenty of dry kindling on hand.

Rule number three: If you want to cook over the fire, start it at least one hour before you plan to prepare your food, so you have a good, hot bed of coals.

Rule number four: A fire needs to breathe, so don't pile the wood on too thickly and smother it.

I prefer the tipi-method of fire building, myself. Start with a little tinder (dry leaves, pine needles, bark, milk-weed fluff, etc. [a purist never uses paper]), then make a tipi of small kindling sticks over the top.

Add another layer of "tipi poles" made of larger sticks, followed by branches larger still, then top it off with a few logs on the outside. I think you get the picture.

When you touch a match to the tinder at the bottom of your tipi, the whole thing should go up in one big whoosh.

I should know, because over the fourth-of-July weekend recently past, I had occasion to build just such a fire for a little cook-out picnic we had here with the family.

After spending all morning dragging branches and kindling down from the woods and chopping it up to fit in my home-made, cement-block barbecue, I laid up a nice, big tipi fire, all ready to light when the relatives arrived.

I got SUCH a big *whoosh* when I touched match to tinder, it singed the hair on my arms and welded together the hair on my head at the ends. I had to trim my locks later that evening in order to get a comb through!

But our food, cooked over the open fire, was well worth it. Nothing else tastes quite like hamburgers and hot dogs prepared over a wood fire.

Course, dropping a few right in the ash does add to the flavor.

> *I do believe I must have a little pyromania in me.*

No picnic would be complete without roasting a few marsh-mallows over the dying coals. I, myself, prefer a lightly-browned marshmallow with a mooshey center, but there are those among us who prefer their sugar-puffs flaming black and crunchy.

I won't go into that whole marshmallow debate in the short space of this column—it could get nasty.

I can't think of anything more soothing than sitting in front of a waning fire and staring at the dying embers. Beats the stomach-turning dramas on TV any day.

In fact, I like watching a fire so much, when I was asked to burn all the debris from our house-building project one evening, I took on the job with gusto. (I do believe I must have a little pyromania in me.)

I watched as plywood pieces, shingle scraps and all manner of building rubbish went up in smoke. Then I added a few more things—my old well cover, a few tires, a huge piece of old carpet.

23

By the time I got done piling on burnables, I had a REALLY *HOT* fire going—so hot, in fact, that you can now call the plastic wrap on the outside of our new house "shrink wrap"—and you may as well just call me "Butch."

Gourmet Adventures

Ever sit on a runway and watch a jumbo-jet drag race?

I had just such an opportunity recently at the Dallas/Fort Worth airport, when the air-traffic controllers' computer system went down. All those jets waiting to land had to keep circling way up there in the Texas sky, while the jets on the ground awaiting takeoff had to stay on terra firma, until all that flight information could get reloaded into the computers, once the system came back "up."

According to our captain, the whole process could take anywhere from one to two hours, so we'd better prepare ourselves to sit on the ground for quite some time before we could get clearance to take off, let alone wait our turn in the long lineup of jets, all eager to do the same thing.

So what do the captains of 127 grounded jumbo jets do while they're waiting for take-off clearance? They jockey for the best runway position, naturally!

From the window seat I occupied on American Airlines flight 1668 from Dallas/Fort Worth to Columbus, I felt as if I were watching a bunch of huge, hungry, slow-motion bugs as they circled for the most advantageous spot to bite the tarmac.

At least in my ring-side seat, I sat securely on the ground while we waited. Up in the sky, I imagine the tension must have been pretty thick in those planes running on fumes by the time they finally got landing clearance.

And how, you might ask, do flight attendants handle a plane load of 150+ disgruntled passengers, strapped into their seats for an unknown amount of time going nowhere?

On the ground, our attendants gave us "Bistro Bags"—an adventure in dining if I ever saw one (you'd have to stretch it to call it gourmet). I imagine the attendants stuck way up there, circling, gave their passengers a diversion more in the line of adult liquid refreshment in order to keep their minds off the fuel gauge.

Now if you ever had the opportunity to fly years ago and remember the kind of five-course dinners airlines used to serve, a Bistro Bag can come as quite a shock.

Back in the 60s and 70s, passengers got things like crab-stuffed tomatoes, lobster thermidor and cherries jubilee. In-flight dining now brings a person face to face with half a shriveled-up ham sandwich on sawdust-white, with a petrified brownie for dessert.

Quite a comedown, to say the least.

The Bistro Bag did have an air of adventure about it, though. Those little hermetically-sealed bags took an advanced engineering degree to open, which did keep most of us occupied for quite a spell.

Then, of course, those of us who finally managed to open the gourmet mustard packs had to spend another 15 minutes cleaning up the yellow stuff that squirted all over the place as we tried to aim that little hole toward the limp lettuce leaf covering our rubbery ham.

Once the lady sitting at the end of our row tried to elicit some sympathy from the flight attendant as he came by, but he waved his hand and said, "Honey, I never eat airline food. I always bring my own lunch!"

It's a good thing we live in this technological wonder of an age. Even though one flip of a plug can bring a whole air-traffic-control system crashing down, at least we have these nifty in-flight phones on the back of each airline seat, so (theoretically, at least) you can call out for pizza!

It's a Cat and Mouse game!
(or In search of a better mouse trap)

Mice, mice, mice. We were overrun with MICE!

Now, I'm as tolerant a person as you'd likely find in this world; when it comes to the old adage, "Live and let live," I've always tried to follow that directive to the best of my ability.

But, let's consider the lowly mouse.

In the country, living next to a State Forest, no less, a body would expect to have a few of those little critters trying to move in every fall when the weather begins to turn nippy.

Hey, they need a warm place to survive, too.

As long as they stayed in the garage or along the foundation of the house, I didn't mind the presence of a mouse or two all that much.

However, when they started running across the deck to stand outside the sliding-glass window smiling at me, I knew they were on the fast path to upgrading their accommodations.

Moving into the house with me meant that I had to draw the line somewhere, right? Of course right! And without resorting to chemical warfare, what better way to control a mouse problem than to get a cat?

Now as a dedicated "dog person" I've always felt that the only practical reason to keep a cat revolved around its unique ability to keep rodent-type critters at bay.

You have to realize, I grew up with a father who contended that the only good cat was a dead cat, so it took me a while to evolve from the mind-set that if you *dared* to have a cat at all, it belonged only in the barn.

Of course, once I made the acquaintance of a cat on a personal basis, I quickly changed my tune about their worth. They can be wonderful companions—especially when the critters begin to move in.

Enter a neighbor with cats to spare, who gladly shared not one, but three felines—two kittens along with their spooky mama. I only needed one cat, really, but how can you say no to a friendly neighbor who delivers?

The hungry babies took up residence in Roxie's dog house and gladly offered their friendship in exchange for regular meals. But, the fearful mother decided she'd had enough the first time she came nose to nose with Chocolate-Lab/Dalmatian/Dingbat Roxie. So Mama Cat hightailed it for home.

I, on the other hand, ended up with two kittens—Bogey and Bacall. No matter, they'd grow. Maybe by spring they'd finally figure out what it meant to catch mice.

Meanwhile, I still had a rodent problem.

I thought to try one of those new, superwammedon sonic blasters that's *supposed* to keep mice, rats, fleas, spiders and other assorted "pests" at bay with high-frequency sound waves.

Nice idea, but in practical application, not so much. One thing is already quite apparent: this device has given "Boots" quite a charge (the 15-year-old Siamese [who wouldn't know a mouse if she tripped over one] that keeps my Aunt company in the house). She runs all over the place jumping at the walls when-ever I turn the thing on!

So much for electronic technology.

In all the homes I've occupied over the years (including this nice, new one at the edge of Mohican Forest), I've done battle with most every rodent-type critter you can imagine—kangaroo mice, field mice, house mice, chipmunks, red squirrels, skunks (I don't think a purist would classify skunks with rodents, however dealing with a skunk does present its own unique challenge).

I think that the most unsettling foes I've ever come up against in these battles for territory had to be the RATS.

A Rat is *not* aesthetically pleasing.

When you have chipmunks or red squirrels take up residence in your attic, it doesn't sound like such a bad thing, does it? Such cute little critters and all. Why they just need a warm place to spend the winter, right?

> *Telling someone you have chipmunks in the attic doesn't sound quite so bad as saying you have rats in the basement.*

Let me tell you, those "cute" critters can make one whale of a mess! But at least telling someone you have chipmunks in the attic doesn't sound quite so bad as saying you have rats in the basement. (Oh, the shame!)

I've seen the day when I had to wage hand-to-hand combat against the basement rats when they decided to take over the first floor of the old farmhouse where I raised my three small children.

"Take that, you dastardly rodent," I said, wielding a handy two-by-four against one that had made it to the top of the basement steps. "I will NOT let you near my babies!" (Even the exterminator said those were the largest rats he'd ever seen.)

Together we put an end to their "coup d'état," however, my little Norfolk Island Pine "ET" was never quite the same, after an attempted midnight raid by their guerilla force which completely un-potted that poor, defenseless sentinel.

You'll be happy to know that ET survived, and now (25 years later) he stands guard near the dining-room window, where he frequently reaches out to grab unsuspecting diners; however, he has retained a deep-seated fear of digging rodents.

Now 'round-about this time, when I'd given up hope of any rodent-catching help this season, another cat began to make its presence known in these parts. Obviously a drop-off, and more obviously, she'd been someone's house cat. She tried her best to zip inside any door opened wide enough to allow her entry.

She was a nice, friendly cat, as cats go. But I already had two kittens, along with my Aunt's old, nearly blind Siamese. I didn't need any more felines. I wasn't about to name this one and begin to get attached.

However, she had other ideas.

Being a resourceful and basically self-sufficient creature, she kept to herself most days, appearing every second or third day with her offering of a mouse, which gave her the self-proclaimed right to take up residence and share in the kittens' repast.

On extremely cold days, she would curl up in the doghouse right along with Bogey and Bacall. Roxie had long since taken up permanent residence inside the basement, so as far as she was concerned, that dog house was up for grabs.

Now, we all know that you can't have just one mouse, and you certainly can't have just one cat, either.

Come spring, the no-name, drop-off cat began to "expand." And when her time was upon her, naturally, she decided to have her kittens in the nice, warm "cat house" (definitely can't call it a dog house any longer).

Five little orange-and-white fur balls. All of a sudden, I had a cat explosion on my hands. What in blazes was I going to do with all these cats?

Well, I'll wait until they get to that "cute" stage and see if I can pawn them off... I mean give them away to some welcoming homes.

The cute stage came and went. The gangly-playful stage came and went. The garage sale with the "Free Kittens" sign came and went, and I managed to find a home for just one kitten.

Eight more cats. And only one of them had made any overture toward catching a mouse—the mama cat, Marmalade. Yes, I finally named her. How could I not? She's a great little mama, and a terrific mouser. Would that she'd train her progeny to learn her mousing skill.

Soooooooo, I couldn't interest you in a lovely, orange-and-white bundle of fur and love, now, could I?

(Please say yes. I don't think I could bear to resort to getting a dog who'll eat cats!)

Laughter: good medicine for a sickly soul

"I love to laugh, ha, ha, he ho! Loud and long and clear... I love to laugh, ho, ho, he, ha! It's getting worse every year!"

Uncle Albert in Mary Poppins had the right idea. Life's too short to dwell on all the "heavy" things that can weigh us down.

So lighten up and laugh!

What? You can't find anything to laugh about, you say? Or even something to help you crack a hint of a smile on that sour-puss of a face?

Then maybe your funny bone needs a little adjustment. Given the quirks of human nature, you certainly don't have to look very far to find SOMETHING funny to make you laugh.

Take, for instance, the antics of a two-year-old. (Granted, if you're the one on 24-7 duty, the job can seem more than a little daunting at times. But for argument's sake, stick with me, here.)

The opportunity has presented itself for me to spend quite a bit of time with my little granddaughter, Lizzie Zink, of late. Being a very active child, she definitely has the ability to keep a household "stirred up!"

The FUN part comes to the fore when she puts her imagination to work—which happens to be most every waking moment. You see, she's seldom ever just Lizzie; she's Dumbo, or Robin Hood, or Black Beauty, or Barney, or Mogly in the Jungle Book, or Zaboomapho (a bouncing lemur, for the uninitiated).

I think you get the idea.

How can a person keep from smiling—or giving an outright guffaw—when such an exuberant child clutches a paper feather in her fist and runs up and down the hallway with a tiny, stuffed, Timothy Mouse perched on her hat, shouting, *"Fly, Dumbo, Fly. Don't drop the magic feather!"*

> *No matter what the situation, humor and laughter can help lighten the load.*

Such a gift can lighten any heart—especially her mother's, whom the obstetrician has ordered to bed to safeguard the next, little Zink struggling his way to make it into this world.

No matter what the situation, humor and laughter can help lighten the load. Sometimes you just have to change your focus a bit in order to see it.

"The more I laugh, he, he ha, ho! The more I fill with glee. And the more the glee, ha, ha, ho, he! The more I'm a merrier me!"

Laughter—it's one of the Creator's greatest gifts to humanity. Think about it, can you name one other creature which possesses such an ability?

I must mention that I HAVE seen a dog smile, on occasion, but I have yet to hear a single snicker or giggle escape from a contented canine.

If you ask me, I think the Creator Himself got the biggest belly laugh after he created man. That's why He had to take the next day off to rest, don'tcha know—because he couldn't stop laughing!!

Norman Cousins, author of, *Anatomy of an Illness As Perceived by the Patient,* credits his life to laughter. He also wrote, *Head First: The Biology of Hope and the Healing Power of the Human Spirit.*

When the medicine of all the doctors and all the specialists fails, why not give laughter a try. It can, indeed, work miracles.

So laugh a little, or at least do your best to crack a smile :-)

If nothing else, it'll make people wonder what you're up to!

… We Cried…

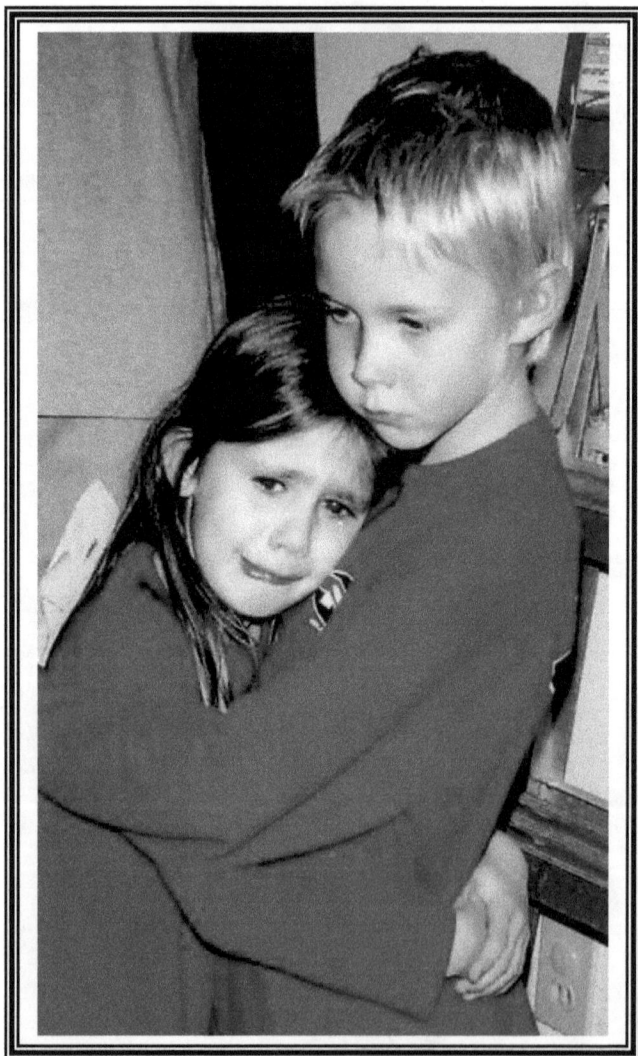

The Sacrificial Deer

It finally happened. I hit a deer. Or rather, a deer hit me, on my way to work.

Try an' figure it—after living in the boonies for 20 years and managing to miss every one that crossed my path, what do I do, but move closer to town and hit one.

They say that the deer you hit comes at you fast, but let me tell you—this happened *FAST!* I had no time to take any evasive action whatsoever. *Blam!* There she was. (Looked like a yearling doe to me.)

Now I don't mean to sound gruesome, but those animals make a mighty BIG bang when they hit. Luckily, with my momentum and her trajectory, the impact threw her away from me instead of up, over the hood and into my windshield.

She bashed in the whole grill and front bumper on my little-red, pick-em-up Ranger.

It's interesting, though. During that lightning-fast incident, I didn't think about damage to the truck (which ended up being substantial) or about getting hurt myself, I focused solely on that ill-fated deer. The instant I saw her stretched out in a dead run, I knew she was a goner.

I've never been that close to a living deer before. If my driver's-side window had been open, I could have reached out and touched her the instant she tried to pass.

But in a split-second, her life came to a screeching halt.

I managed to stop the truck without running into anything else, although I did leave a considerable amount of rubber on the road. Immediately, I got out of the truck and hurried to the edge of the ditch to check on the deer. She was still breathing, but she made no other move. I wanted to jump right down there to comfort her.

"Think, girl; this is a wild animal—a badly *hurt*, wild animal. Don't be stupid." I stood, gaping. I had never watched a deer die.

> "Think, girl; this is a wild animal—a badly hurt, wild animal. Don't be stupid."

Oh, living here in Holmes County I've seen many-a-dead deer, and I've even taken part in the butchering of quite a few. Venison is one of the best meats around, harvested and handled correctly. But I had never killed one before.

I'm told that when the ancient native hunted and killed a deer, he would thank the animal's spirit for giving its life in order that The People might live. This animal wasn't going to contribute to the sustenance of anyone's life. She was a sacrifice to the great god Progress, pure and simple.

I stood at the edge of that ditch and apologized for ending her life.

In a matter of minutes, it was all over. I turned back to my truck to assess the damage, then started hoofing it to the nearest telephone to call the Sheriff's department in order to report my run-in. *(This happened well before carrying cell phones became popular.)*

Upon returning to the accident scene, I waited most of a half-hour for a Sheriff's deputy to arrive, then I filed a damage report, he said I was good to go, and continued on my way.

Luckily, I could still drive the truck, damaged though it be. Only when I finally arrived at work did the shakes begin to hit.

Crises I can handle—it's afterward that I turn into a bowl of Jell-O®.

My editor will tell you I wasn't worth a whit for the rest of the day. I "spun my wheels" all morning, producing next to nothing in the way of useable copy, then at lunch time, I went out to track down insurance estimates.

Now you wouldn't think a lone deer could do all that much damage to a pickup-truck, of all things, would you? But I have to tell you, the estimated cost to fix that damage came as a shock.

Thank heaven for friendly insurance men—and for under-standing editors.

After all my years of uneventful driving, I wondered what it would be like to actually hit something.

Now I know.

I also know one other thing: a deer has very long eye lashes.

My heart will go on and on

May Day! ... - - - ... May Day!

Can you tell me, is the Morse Code for "SOS" three dots, three dashes and three more dots, or is it three dashes, three dots and three more dashes? We dyslexics have trouble remembering this sort of thing.

Having just watched *Titanic*, you'd think that I'd know the answer to that question, wouldn't you? But the truth of the matter is, I've collided with my own iceberg of sorts, and in the aftermath of losing my heart, all manner of practical information has gone right out of my head.

It's not that the loss itself has brought with it a completely unbearable pain—heartache is not unfamiliar territory for me. Heaven knows I've had ample preparation in that department.

The iceberg that's brought me to a screeching halt comes from the shock of a having another close relationship go sour—one that I thought had been based on the kind of love and commitment that works through the craggy ice-crystals of difficulty, not one that sinks at the first sign of damage.

It caught me completely off-guard. No iceberg warnings at all. But looking back, I now recognize danger signals I should have heeded. (Talk about being asleep in the radio room!)

So now it's just me in my little dinghy, once again paddling like crazy to keep from being sucked down by the undertow.

Where do I go from here?

I go on. That's the way of things in this life. Like Rose in that classic tale of lost love and disaster, I, too, must choose to live, rather than let my heart die a frosty death.

We do have a choice, don'tcha' know: when loss and disappointment come our way we can either wallow in self-pity (and

turn into a curmudg-
eon no one wants to
associate with), or we
can get on with the
business of living.

> *When loss and disappointment come our way we can either wallow in self-pity... or we can get on with the business of living.*

That's not to say there's no time for grief. On the contrary, working through grief is an important step in the whole process of getting on with life.

When I reel from the pain of loss, however, the thought of becoming a hermit does hold a certain romantic appeal—like ol' Johnny Weimer, the neighborhood hermit of my childhood days, who supposedly espoused the life of a recluse after he was jilted at the altar.

Strange man, Johnny. He kept entirely to himself, making only a monthly trip to town on his Ford tractor to get supplies. Rumor had it he subsisted entirely on rolled-up pancakes he carried around in his pockets. (Unrequited love can drive a person to do funny things.)

I don't know that I could stomach a steady diet of pocket pancakes, but I have been known to resort to the solace of a whole batch of chocolate-chip cookies, on occasion.

I guess the real test of survival comes only when we face our icebergs, and either we deal with them until they're cut into manageable pieces, or the weight of the whole thing drags us down.

By the way would anyone happen to be in need of any ice? I have quite a big supply of cubes here, and no good place to keep them in this little tipi, in which I've taken up residence.

(Do you think, perhaps, I should take up the potter's wheel, now, too?)

MaryLee's Misty Shadow

Warning: If you're not a dog person and you can't stomach much "schmaltz," don't bother reading this column any further.

Only those of us completely captivated by a dog can begin to understand the eccentricities that evolve when it comes to caring for man's (or in this case woman's) most faithful friend.

Dogs come and dogs go over a person's lifetime, but once in a while, one particular dog comes along who manages to steal your heart.

When a wiggly, six-week-old Black Labrador Retriever puppy entered my life about 14 years ago, little did I know then how fully I would come to depend on my "Misty Shadow."

I have to tell you, I'm one of those people who's mothered everything from bumb lambs to orphaned possums. (Yes, even baby possums are ugly.) So when this tiny, whiny, too-young-to-be-away-from-her-mother, black fur-ball came to me, naturally, I had to fill in.

Misty cried that first night away from her Mama, just as any normal puppy would, so I put a hot water bottle under a fuzzy blanket to make a cozy spot for her.

No good. She kept crying. I wound up an old alarm clock and tucked it under there, too—that trick had calmed countless other puppies in the past, but it didn't work on Misty.

Nothing I tried eased her whining, until I finally curled up on the floor beside her. Then Misty snuggled in and slept. But whenever I'd stir to get up, she'd waken and start crying all over again. You guessed it; I spent the next several nights sleeping on the floor with Misty.

She had me.

From that portentous beginning, Misty trained me well, and I came to depend on the company of my steadfast friend as much as she depended on mine.

She loves to "go" with me, no matter where I head to. When she hears my keys jingle, Misty makes a beeline to the truck. Except when we go to the vet's office. Somehow she always knows that destination before I have the tailgate down.

When she became arthritic and ended up with one bumb leg, we adapted our "loading procedure" so she could still get in and out of the truck. I made a step out of an old crate, and Misty would make the jump to the truck bed in stages.

Those times when I couldn't take her along with me, she'd crawl into her doghouse and pout. I'd give her a dog-biscuit treat when I left, but invariably, she'd never touch it until I came back home. Only when I returned would she eat that biscuit—whether it be 10 hours or 10 days later.

Like all Labrador Retrievers, Misty loves water. The first time she saw a pond, it puzzled her, but when I waded in to swim and called her to follow me, it didn't take her long to figure out what to do. From then on, if she could find a puddle, she'd try to swim in it.

The place I live now has a perfect little "swimmin' hole" back in the Horsetail Run, where Misty loves to take a dip. But since she's nearly blind now, I have to lead her there. She won't wander to the woods on her own any more unless she can hear my voice to guide her way.

Misty has moved four times with me; she's endured countless other pesky dogs and cats (and kids) in the menageries I've had over the years; she's given birth to 16 puppies of her own. (Motherhood was definitely not her cup of tea!)

In time, all the other dogs and cats and lambs and kids have grown or gone on, but Misty and I remain. Together we've lived through 14 difficult years of upheaval.

Through all the changes, I've been the only constant in Misty's life, so perhaps that explains her unequaled devotion. But if the truth be known, it is Misty who has really been the only constant in mine. I can hardly bear the thought of going on without her.

One deer season she disappeared for three days, and I figured she'd been shot; but I found her, under a shed. She'd crawled into

41

> *If the truth be known, it is Misty who has been the only constant through all the changes in my life.*

a hole under there and got stuck in her panic to get away from the gunshots.

(Misty's terrified of guns.)

Four years ago, she disappeared; I figured she crawled off into the woods to die, but a week later she came back—three-legged and hungry.

Three years ago, I wouldn't have bet you two cents that she'd live through the winter; since then she's seen three more winters.

But last weekend she awoke to find another leg gone bad, leaving just two good ones—and both of those on the same side. Now, instead of walking with a limp, she has a decided list to the starboard. Misty could hardly get up, let alone walk; even so, she tried to jump into the truck as I got ready to leave.

Her body may be wasting away, but her spirit continues to bounce like that of a pup.

Today, Misty moved as well as she has in months—another amazing recovery. I'll bet I've buried that dog 10 times in my mind over the past year.

She keeps surprising me.

I know Misty's light grows dim, and the time comes soon when I'll have to say goodbye to my faithful friend. But perhaps, MaryLee's Misty Shadow won't be that far away, after all.

Shadows never do get very far, now, do they?

The BIGGIE Questions

Who am I? Why am I here? Where am I going?

Whenever life pulls the rug out from under a body, it does tend to make one ponder such gigantic, universal questions, while lying there in the dust, gasping for breath.

Having your world come crashing down around your ears can leave you feeling overwhelmed and hopeless, feeling vulnerable and alone.

Listen, friend, it happens to the best of us—and more often than *any* of us would care to admit. I can tell you one thing from personal experience: when you're lying there, trying to figure out what in blazes happened, there's only one direction to look—UP!

Things WILL get better, but it does take a little time for the dust to settle.

While I can offer no sure-fire methods for replacing that slippery rug, nor explain how or why it got pulled out from under you in the first place, I *CAN* offer some effective techniques to help you find a little sure-footing while piecing the fragments of a shattered life back together.

Lord knows I've had plenty of experience piecing this Cracked-pot back together often enough.

1) Look forward! Do not focus on where you've been or on what has gone wrong; instead keep those eyes straight ahead. Believe me, I know that's much easier said than done, but it's *absolutely essential* to make yourself focus on something positive, rather than on the negative circumstances that have led you to your present, dust-eating position.

2) Find something constructive to do for yourself: Take a class, build a birdhouse, write a story, crochet an afghan, pull weeds in the garden, clean out a closet, change the oil in the truck, climb a tree and sing a song at the top of your lungs, or take a walk and revel in the healing energy nature has to offer.

Choose something that pleases you, that feeds you, that makes you feel proud of the accomplishment. If you're limited physically, work within your parameters. Find something constructive—and preferably creative—to help you *begin* to move forward, instead of sitting there, scribbling in the dust.

I think you get the idea.

What's that? You say you can't possibly take any time for yourself? That you have too many people depending on you, too many responsibilities, too many chores to attend to?

Poppycock, I say! If you don't MAKE time to care for yourself, to take care of filling your own needs, how can you possibly have the inner resources to care for anyone else?

Nobody else can heal your hurts or live your life for you; no one else is responsible for filling your needs. *You* must do whatever it takes to put your life back together again.

Which brings us to number:
3) Begin a "wish list" and divide your list into three parts:
     a) Things I want to learn;
     b) Things I'd like to do or have;
     c) and Places I want to go before I die.

Write down everything you can think of, no matter how crazy or off-the-wall it may sound to anyone else. Put it down there in black and white. Begin to give it life by acknowledging the desire buried deep within.

By the way, if you think this exercise is too selfish a thing to do, think again; those desires were put there for a reason.

Whether you *think* you can attain everything on the list is irrelevant at this point. What's important right now is to write it all down.

Once you have this master list, go back over it and choose two things you can focus upon in the next year. Of those two, choose one that you can put energy into *right now*.

Brainstorm for ways you can bring that particular item into fruition—and once again, write down everything, no matter how wild and crazy it may sound. Often the most unlikely methods turn out to be the most promising and workable, after all.

If you haven't guessed it by now, this exercise should begin to awaken your awareness of the many possibilities open to you, no matter how dire your circumstances may feel at the moment. It also helps in setting new priorities for your life, in determining what's really important, what's *not*, and showing you that you do have choices.

By the way, don't throw that wish list away. Save it. Then next year— and five years from now, and ten years from now—pull it back out to take stock of how far you've come. Check off what you've accomplished and re-determine the direction you'd like to keep going.

> *When you set positive energy into motion, wonderful things can happen!*

You might be interested to know that the list I began nine years ago has more than half of the items crossed off already— and those check marks happen to fall beside what I originally thought to be the most impossible dreams of all!

Hey, when you set positive energy into motion, wonderful things can happen.

Where intention goes, energy flows!

The "bag of miracles" is open to everyone, but it takes faith and ACTION to reach in and begin to give life to those miracles. It takes grit, the ability to look forward, and unflagging determination to make your life worth living again.

O.K., I'm working on another new list myself: go on an archeological dig; spend summers at the sea shore; take up jewelry-making; learn to make stained-glass windows; raise black sheep, build a greenhouse...

...say, you wouldn't happen to know anyone who has set of used bagpipes for sale, would you?

Empty Nest

From the moment a squalling baby bursts into the world and changes your life, you know that it's coming—the empty nest.

When they're tiny, you think they'll *never* sleep through a whole night, or learn how to dress themselves, or eat a whole meal without spilling something.

They learn to walk, then run, and suddenly you're watching them climb onto the school bus. Before you know it they're donning cap and gown and reaching for a diploma.

Along the way, we have a few chances to practice the steps in letting them go: we nervously send Jimmy off to his first day in Kindergarten, then for a whole week at summer camp; we live through the tension of Sally's first softball game during her tomboy years, then she's fluffing and primping to get ready for her first prom.

And Katie, bless her heart, gets nursed through all the bumps and broken bones of her horse-loving stage (which never ends), until suddenly you look up, and she's packing her boom-box and heading off to college.

When they're adorable toddlers, you can't imagine living any kind of a life without them, but after listening to two, teen-aged girls argue with their brother (for three hours straight) over who left the cap off the toothpaste, the prospect of having them move out on their own does *not* seem quite so daunting.

I firmly believe that God invented "the teen years" so parents would not have such a hard time letting go. I'm also convinced that—if we're lucky—He gives us children in the first place so we can learn how to really live. As they learn from us, we also learn from them.

We get to enjoy them for a few, hectic years alive with activity, then eventually, each bird must grow up and learn how to fly.

My kids have given me so much sunshine, I can't imagine what life would have been like without them. Granted, they've given me a lot of pain and frustration and aggravation along the way, too. But in the overall balance, sunshine comes out on top.

> *I believe that God invented "the teen years" so parents would not have such a hard time letting go.*

So, now that they're all "flying on their own," I must find some other way to fill my life without relying on their constant presence to get me from one day into the next.

I can't hide behind a child sitting on my lap, anymore.

Not an easy challenge. But then, no challenge ever comes easy, does it?

These "life changes" can be a little scary, but scary is all right—even exhilarating—if you go into them with the right attitude.

For the first time in my life, I am not responsible for taking care of another human being. It's just me, my old blind/lame/deaf dog and a crazy cat with a water fixation.

It takes some getting used to, this living alone, but I'm adjusting. You see, it's finally my turn to fly.

What every woman should have and know

IN HER LIFETIME EVERY WOMAN SHOULD HAVE:

- one indecent proposal to refuse, so she can know what it feels like to be desired;

- at least one honorable proposal to accept, so she can know what it feels like to be honored;

- a love she's content to have left behind, and another she wishes never got away;

- a past that's juicy enough to look forward to retelling in her old age (as long as she can clean it up enough to tell her grandchildren).

EVERY WOMAN WANTS:

- at least one piece of furniture she's chosen for herself that wasn't previously owned by anyone else in her family;

- the perfect ball-gown for a formal affair in which she feels like a knockout; one that will stop conversation when she walks into the room;

- a matching dinner set for eight that includes crystal goblets, cloth napkins, and a mouth-watering recipe for a meal that will astonish her guests and leave them wanting more (which she could serve in that perfect ball gown!).

EVERY WOMAN NEEDS:

- a crescent wrench, a cordless drill, and a black lace push-up bra that makes her look like a million bucks;

- enough money within her control to rent her own place, even if she thinks she'll never want to, or never need to;

- one friend who always makes her laugh, lets her cry, and listens to her whine without passing judgment;

- at least one good dog, one good pickup truck, and a complete set of Mary Kay makeup.

EVERY WOMAN SHOULD KNOW:

▪ the confidence it takes to quit a job, or break up with a lover;

▪ the ecstasy of falling in love, completely losing herself in the process;

▪ the satisfaction of falling in love WITHOUT completely losing herself (and if she's lucky, it's all with the same mate).

EVERY WOMAN SHOULD LEARN:

▪ how to confront a friend without ruining the friendship;

▪ how to argue with her mother and still keep peace in the family.

EVERY WOMAN SHOULD ACCEPT:

▪ that she can't change the width of her hips, the size of her feet, or the nature of her parents;

▪ that her childhood may not have been perfect, but it's over;

▪ that she has to ride out the consequences of the choices she's made;

▪ the experience of living alone, even if she doesn't necessarily like it.

EVERY WOMAN NEEDS TO KNOW:

▪ what she can and can't accomplish in a day, a month, and a year;

▪ whom she can trust, whom she can't, and why she shouldn't take it personally;

▪ where to go to refresh her soul, whether it be a walk on the beach, a talk with her best friend, or spending two years living in a tipi.

At least once in her life, every woman should grasp the power of feeling in control of her destiny, as well as the powerlessness and utter vulnerability of knowing that the universe wields final authority over all.

This woman knows that although friendships come, and companionships go, saying the ultimate goodbye to anyone never comes easy, no matter how fleeting your time together in the grand scheme of things.

And so, I must say goodbye, Mr. TreeMan. May you continue to sow seeds of benevolence in the next great adventure. Here's hoping the Lord has lots of trees in His garden.

Mary had a little lamb

Actually, Mary had several lambs over the years, but way back in the third grade, Frisky started off the whole lineup of little woolies.

You see, Frisky lost his mama at birth, so he needed a substitute. And since farmer Dad (who wasn't crazy about sheep to begin with) didn't have the time to waste on a bumb lamb, and Mom already had her hands full taking care of four kids, guess who qualified as surrogate mom?

You guessed it—me.

At the ripe old age of eight I was already a sucker for taking on seemingly hopeless tasks (a failing that's led me on many a hair-raising adventure ever since, I can tell you).

By adopting Frisky as my very own, it set the tone for the way I've chosen pets ever since. I gravitate toward the shy puppy, the fearful kitten, or the lost and hurting strays who need someone to love them.

You know, many of the people in my life fit that category, too!

My best friend calls it the "Wounded Bird Syndrome," an affliction common among us Pollyanna types who want to save the world.

I knew it was up to me to keep Frisky among the living, so every day, three or four times a day, I'd hustle out to the barn with milk bottle in hand. He'd always be there, waiting.

Before long he grew big enough to eat grain and hay, and big enough to butt the nipple right out of the bottle. (He covered us both in milk on more than one occasion.) And even when he no longer needed the bottles, he'd still stand at the barnyard gate, hollering for them.

We kept Frisky separated from the rest of sheep at first, because the other mamas would butt him away whenever he began searching for a snack. He wasn't big enough to defend himself by a long shot.

After he finally gained a little size, Frisky joined his peers in the pasture. By that time the bigger ewes left him alone, and he could jump and cavort with the other spring lambs to his heart's content.

Discovering the world is a heady business.

Every afternoon when I stepped off the school bus, Frisky met me at the end of our long lane (on his side of the pasture fence, of course), and he followed me all the way up to the house and barn, bleating for his dinner the whole trip.

One day when I got off the bus, Frisky didn't meet me. I immediately sensed something was wrong and ran the whole quarter-mile lane without stopping.

> *Discovering the world is a heady business.*

No Frisky in the barnyard, and no Frisky in his usual pen, either. But when I walked out behind the barn, I found my lamb in a cold, stiff heap. Dad said all the bigger rams had butted him to death.

Against so many, my motherless lamb never stood a chance.

It was my first soul-shattering experience with death, and I'm afraid to say, I did not handle it at all well. I ran to the house, flew up the stairs and threw myself face down on the bed in hysterics. I moped around for days.

Before long, my Mother's sage wisdom brought me back to reality, and she helped me to understand that "everybody needs to learn how to lose." (A lesson I've held in valuable stead over this harrowing and bumpy path of mine.)

One of my favorite poems contains a line that says, *"...after a while you learn to accept your defeats with the grace of an adult, not the grief of a child."*

This week I say good-bye to the faithful companion who's shared the past 14 tumultuous years of my life. Misty's body finally gave out, even though her heart and her spirit still beat strong.

I'll miss my Misty Shadow. But I believe she'll come bounding up to welcome me when I, too, pass through that veil onto the other side. She'll be right there at the head of my animal welcoming committee—right next to Frisky.

Paddling with one oar in the water

"He's a few bricks short of a load; the light's on but nobody's home; she's a bubble off plumb; his elevator works, but it doesn't stop on all floors."

Recognize any of those little ditties? You've probably heard those and many more just like them. When it comes to one's mental processes, we have a way of trivializing a person's shortcomings with such wisecracks, but in truth, mental illness is no laughing matter.

According to the National Institute of Mental health, clinical depression alone (just one of many illnesses affecting one's mental processes) affects more than 17 million Americans a year, yet more than half of those people suffer without seeking treatment of any kind.

One out of every five adults experiences a severe bout with depression at some point in his life, and depression affects twice as many women as men.

But the term "depression" misleads a lot of folks. Feeling sad and downhearted at some of the monkey-wrenches life can throw at a person is NORMAL. But the long-term mental and physical degeneration of a full-blown Clinical Depression persists long after any said monkey-wrench has been dealt with.

If left untreated, the severe pain of depression can even lead a person to suicide.

The good news is: *you DON'T HAVE to suffer; help IS available.* More than 80% of those affected by this sneaky disease can respond to treatment. But you must SEEK help in order to find relief.

And help comes in many forms to deal with the psychological, emotional and physical manifestations of depression, as well as the chemical imbalances. (Does depression create those imbalances, or do the imbalances cause depression—it's the old "chicken or egg" question; no one knows which comes first.)

How do you know if clinical depression affects you? Do you:

    1) feel hopeless and helpless most of the time?
    2) have far less energy than normal?
    3) have difficulty doing things that used to be easy?
    4) feel worthless?
    5) feel irritable and anxious?
    6) cry a lot?

Have you:

    7) lost motivation to do the things you once enjoyed?
    8) noticed your sleep patterns changing?
    9) lost your appetite?
    10) Do you feel that life is just not worth living anymore?

If you recognized yourself (or someone you love) in more than three of the above symptoms, don't waste time—*seek help immediately!*

You don't have to let the black dog of depression continue to nip at your heels.

And let me stress this—*there is no shame in seeking help.* Contrary to what the uninformed believe, it takes great courage to seek help. "There is great wisdom in counsel," goes the old, Proverbial saying.

If you don't know where to go, or how to seek help, take the first step by going to a Depression Screening Site for evaluation. Call the National Depression Screening Day Hot Line to find the location nearest you. This service is free and anonymous—and it can change your life.

As one who's paddled through the rock-strewn rapids of Clinical Depression, I can testify that although you may feel a bit waterlogged during the ride leading to calmer waters, you WILL find a peaceful harbor and begin to enjoy life once more.

Now when people accuse me of "rowing with one oar in the water" I can laugh and agree with them, and even enjoy making a big splash!

You'll laugh again, too—I promise.

For those who wait

"Dear Crackpot:

*Thank you so very much for your recent article con-
cerning mental illness.... How about a column for those
of us who stand on the sidelines of the mentally ill?"*

For you, my anonymous friend, I take pause from my usual
tongue-in-cheek style to address your concerns and let you know
that you do not stand alone in your apprehensive vigil.

For you, who must stand on the other side of the locked door
and submit to searches before the staff will admit you to see a
loved one in the protective environment of a psychiatric unit, I
have the most enduring respect.

For you, who must try to explain what's happening to your
friends and neighbors (especially when you don't really understand it all yourself) I pray for continued enlightenment and dip-
lomacy. You need not feel ashamed.

Whatever you do, don't fall into the "what-will-other-people-
think" trap. Those who judge most harshly lack knowledge. You
can educate them. As my ol' English professor used to say,
"there's no shame in ignorance, just in stupidity."

Enlighten my ignorance, but forgive my stupidity.

For you, who must chauffeur your loved ones to regular ap-
pointments, remind them to take their medication and live with
the paranoia and uncertainty of such imbalance, I salute your
steadfastness.

I strongly encourage you to take charge of filling your own
needs. When you are the stable one the family tends to lean on,
it's doubly important that you do not let your *entire* life revolve
around the needs of everyone else around you.

Find some creative outlet for yourself—something you really
enjoy or want to learn—and make time to DO it. The most important aspect in survival for your whole family, is keeping yourself filled and whole.

You can't afford to fall apart when those around you do.

And when you look at your children and live with the fear that the increased tendency for mental illness often runs in families, I offer this ray of hope: you can teach your children how to avoid the prospect of mental imbalance in their own lives by showing them practical ways to deal with their feelings and fears now.

Teach them that it's all right to let their feelings out, and show them appropriate ways to deal with those feelings. Keeping negative emotions like anger and hate and

The fear of something tends to grow the more we run from it. But when we face our fear squarely, it finally loses its power over us.

shame all bottled-up inside can trigger the biochemical cocktail that often trips a mental short-circuit.

Think of fear as the bully who uses intimidation to get a little kid's lunch money. When that little kid finally figures out that a getting a black eye is no worse than going hungry, he'll stand up to that bully. And when he does, the chance will be very good that the bully will be the one to go hungry next time.

Teach your children to ask themselves, "What's the worst thing that can happen in this situation?" Then show them how to brainstorm and come up with as many answers to deal with each circumstance as they can. When you spell out practical ways to deal with a difficulty, it seems far less frightening. (Sometimes an off-the-wall idea even turns out to be the best solution.)

Also encourage your children to create. Give them the opportunity to express themselves in many ways. When you do, you'll find remarkable people emerging through such creativity, and you'll be teaching them that it's all right to become a whole, vital, thinking human being.

In that becoming, they will learn to avoid the pitfalls that may be pre-programmed into their body chemistry, and they will learn healthier ways to interact with the world.

And lastly, for you, who cope with threats of suicide or must deal with delusions or hallucinations (no, the TV isn't emitting X-rays, the garage door opener won't beam you up, and the neighbor's cat is not out to take vengeance on you personally) I give my deepest and most profound admiration for your unwavering loyalty.

Very few emotionally shattered people have that kind of unconditional support. And I can tell you from experience, it's mighty hard to "make your way back" without it. Such devotion can cost the stable person dearly, but I know its immeasurable value.

It also helps if you have a brother who's not averse to throwing a pie now and again! *(It's a long story; someday I'll tell it.)* Sometimes it takes an extraordinary form of encouragement to let a loved one know that everything will be "normal" again.

Also know this—that no matter what happens, you are not personally responsible for the decisions that another person makes, even though you may be deeply affected by them. You still have control over your own responses to any given situation.

You don't have to let threats manipulate you.

If, after standing faithfully by, you finally come to the place where you can no longer cope with your situation, seek help yourself—*immediately!* That's what it's there for.

When you wake up in the morning to face (as you say) another day of the "nightmare reality," remember that you do not tread this path alone—no matter how alone you may feel at times. Seek out the counsel of a competent professional and the encouraging support of those in similar circumstances.

> *There's always a way through the dark tunnel, and I can testify that you will find light at the other end.*

Any professional worth his salt will work out a payment plan you can handle. Don't ever let lack of money stop you from seeking help this important.

There's always a way through the dark tunnel, and I can testify that you will find light at the other end.

Above all else, do everything possible to keep your sense of humor intact. The ability to laugh at life's foibles is vital in this somber struggle for sanity.

If you can't find anything in your own life to laugh about, then watch an old "Laurel and Hardy" slapstick comedy or read one of Robert Fulghum's books.

I guarantee they'll make you laugh!

No matter what triggers a healthy belly laugh for you—DO IT. It's good medicine for the soul.

(By the way, if you need a good chocolate-cream pie to add an exclamation point to your comic relief, I know right where you can find one!)

Open letter and Tribute to John Denver

Dear John, (no, it's not one of *those* letters!)

I need to thank you and let you know how much your music has meant to me. You have always had the uncanny capacity to reflect exactly what I feel. And after reading your autobiography, *Take Me Home*, I now know why.

Thank you, too, for being so open and honest. Looking at one's true reflection is not easy.

The similarities in the paths we have trod amaze me, though they should not. Oh, I'm not talking fame and notoriety by a long shot—rather the inner turmoil and quest for a calming center that we've both sought in the midst of life's raging tempests.

You and I share not only the same kind of beginnings (constraints of mid-west, dutiful mind-sets and the upheaval of military life) but also the same kind of struggles and fears in our constant striving to find out who we really are.

I can't help but shake my head in amazement when I realize that your major turning points coincided to the very same years with mine. No wonder the things you sang about so accurately reflected my own yearnings and pain.

One particular time in my life stands out above all the others as an example of the healing power in your music. In 1982, after years of upheaval and emotional bankruptcy, to say that I fell apart when my first marriage did, is an understatement.

At that same time, your album *Seasons of the Heart* came to me, and I literally wore that record out, playing it over and over and over again. Like a soothing balm, every song on that album calmed my shattered soul. I can remember sitting in front of a jigsaw puzzle, struggling to make sense of the pieces, while listening to you sing for hours on end.

In the process of fitting that puzzle together, I began piecing my life back together, too. Your music played a vital part in helping me to find my own path, rather than trying to live by someone else's.

"I had to go through there, to get to here."

I've had to live through several hells to realize that. And in each of those hells, your music—in all its phases of stretching and growth—has been a constant beacon for me.

During these ensuing years I've learned that only when you let go of your dreams, do you finally give them the power to find you. And in doing so, I've managed to realize several of mine—including riding in a hot-air balloon and swimming with the dolphins.

> *I've already been singing with you all these years. I don't need to stand on a stage to accomplish that.*

One other big dream remains: I've always wanted to sing with John Denver. But after reading your book, I realized something: I've already been singing with you all these years. I don't need to stand on a stage to accomplish that.

Thank you for helping me to grow. And thank you for showing me that finding the way home is as simple as looking into my own soul. I, too, am finally beginning to understand that reaching my destination is not nearly so important as my journey to get there.

That's not to say it's a trip without peril. And if I should happen to lose my way, I need only listen to your music to guide me gently back.

On Sunday, Oct. 12, 1997, John Denver left this world when the small, experimental plane he was flying crashed into Monterey Bay, just south of San Francisco, California.

John Denver established the *Windstar Foundation*, an environmental activist group, which strives to focus the world's attention on the ever-shrinking resources of this, our earthly home. His most obvious gift—that of his music—continues to light the way for many a wandering mortal as it guides one ever "onward and upward."

I do not mean to immortalize John Denver with this tribute. He was just as human as any of us—and that held the key to his great influence: he was never afraid to let that humanity show.

Perhaps in my own Crackpot way, I have striven to accomplish the same kind of purpose with this column, as John Denver did with his music. He let us know that even though it hurts to struggle over life's hurdles, as long as you stick to your own path, it *will*—eventually—lead you back home.

"Hey it's good, to be back home again!"

A Daddy's Girl Remembers

My Daddy fell down! How could that happen?

Daddies don't fall down—they're giants. They stand tall and carry little girls when they can't walk anymore. Little girls fall down all the time. Not Daddies.

I can't believe my Daddy would fall down. But he did. He didn't see that tree root, and he tripped right over it.

My Daddy fell down.

(This monumental event became a young child's turning point: to imagine, Daddies can actually fall down, too! Who would ever have guessed such a thing could be true?)

"What are you doing in there, girl?"

"Just eating, Dad."

"Well, why don't you come out to the table and eat with me?"

She shuffled slowly to the breakfast nook and shyly put down her plate of eggs with the broken yolks.

"Why were you eating in there all by yourself?"

"Cuz I didn't want you to see all the eggs I ruined trying to fry two perfect eggs for you, Daddy."

"So that's what took so long to get my breakfast this morning without your mother here."

"I never made flipped eggs before. Mom always does that part, and I broke three before I got one to come out right."

"Don't you know I've eaten plenty of broken eggs before?"

"But I thought they had to be perfect for you, Daddy—cuz you're DAD."

(This watershed memory showed a growing girl no one expects perfection all the time—not even Daddies.)

"Pop? Are you awake?" She tip-toed up the steps just after midnight, shaking in her boots and trying not to waken the whole house.

"What's wrong, daughter," came the sleep-foggy voice from behind the bedroom door.

"I had a little trouble with the car, Pop. I thought I'd better tell you before you saw it in the morning."

"What happened? Are you O.K.?"

"I'm fine. Nobody got hurt. But the front fender doesn't look so good."

"Don't worry about it. I'll take a look tomorrow and see what we have to do to fix it."

"O.K., Pop…. Daddy? Thanks for not hollering at me."

"As long as no one got hurt, it's no big deal. Now go to bed and get some sleep. We'll handle it all in the morning."

(This surprising revelation gave a contrite teenager a new appreciation for the growing responsibilities of adulthood and showed her that things are, after all, just things: "How could he roll over and go back to sleep when I wrecked the car? I can't believe he didn't yell at me!")

"Hello? Sis? It's about Dad. I think you'd better sit down."

"What's wrong? What happened?"

"Don't worry, he's doing O.K. He's in the hospital right now."

"Tell me what happened!"

"Daddy had a stroke, and it paralyzed his left side."

"How's Mom? Is she all right?"

"She's doing pretty well. But she has her hands full trying to convince Dad he has to stay in bed. He thinks there's a stranger in the bed with him, and he keeps trying to get up."

"As soon as I can get a baby-sitter for the kids, I'll be right there. Tell Mom I'm on my way."

(This life-altering catastrophe marked the first time a young adult really understood that life, indeed, is fragile: "How could a strapping, I-can-do-damn-near-anything farmer have been cut down in the flower of his prime?")*

* * * * *

(30+ years later)

I've sat death-watch at my father's bedside before; we maintain a special bond—a spark of deep remembrance—that binds us to each other through lifetimes spent exploring the multi-dimensional layers of creation.

Saying goodbye never gets any easier, and yet... we've always been bound so tightly in spirit, I don't feel that terrible "cutting away." We come to each other again and again on life's byways—different times, different places, but always in a relationship of unconditional love.

Regardless of the driving forces that carried him forward, the one, overriding motivation of this lifetime remained building a family. "Nothing else lasts. Nothing else endures."

The children and the children's children we leave behind, carry forward the legacy left us by those who came before—from the cattle rustlers of the Scottish lowlands, down through the generations to men like Great-Grandpa Johnston, Uncle George, and now Daddy—Farmers to the end, husbandmen of the clan that raises up ever more ornery hell-raisers and characters with each generation.

We thank you, we honor you, we love you, and we call you blessed.

Though your physical presence may be missing from the remainder of our life-walks here, we can carry on knowing that you're opening up a new chapter on the other side of the veil—and no doubt giving them holy hell in the process. (Did you enter the next dimension holding your breath there, too?)

Pave the way for us, Dad. We'll meet you at those Pearly Gates (unless you've turned them into airplanes, the way you did the leaf of your mother's dining room table).

65

Daddies, Fathers, Papas, Dads. Without their strengths, without their weaknesses, without the lessons their struggles and misfortunes teach us, we could never hope to become whole ourselves.

"Thanks, Dad," for helping me find my way through the struggles of this life. And thanks for showing me that just when I think I finally have someone figured out, that's when he's apt to surprise me most!

* Preceding portion previously published; material following asterisk added later.

The Wounded Bird
By MaryLee Marilee

Sufferers of the "bird" disease
share this one common thing:
We gather to us wounded birds
to mend their broken wings.

Now those who've handled injured birds
know the uncertainty
of how to treat a wild one's wound,
not deepen injury.

We first must assuage its fear,
work hard its trust to gain;
then gently, softly mesmerize
to draw away its pain.

Before that bird knows what's transpired
our patient has recovered.
He's fit to ply his wings once more,
to flit and fly and flutter.

This little bird has gained my heart,
how can I let him go?
How can I watch him fly away
now that I love him so?

Should I hold tight to make him mine?
Dare I put him in a cage?
I tried that once, and watched it fade,
kept unwilling hostage.

"Open your hand and let him fly,
to choose he must be free;
Only with option to return
can he really belong to me."

That first, bruised bird I tried to patch
was quick to fly away
the instant that his door swung wide.
I cried, and watched, and waved.

The next marred bird I tried to treat
Again, I held too tight.
At first he seemed enthralled with me;
soon I suffered from his bite.

That wounded bird did fly away
to other nests of solace;
he left me with a jagged wound,
a bitter taste of his malice.

Yet, one more bird came to my care,
its wound too deep for sight;
I did not make the same mistake
of grasping this one tight.

To this, the dearest bird of all
I gave autonomy.
He misinterpreted restraint
as uncaring apathy.

I gave him room to spread his wings
in unrestricted skies.
I waited for his heart to mend,
for love to fill his eyes.

I offered my imperfect heart
to share his wounds and pain.
He could not manage such a trust;
it shattered once again.

Far from this lonely nest of mine
my birds all found new life.
Not one is left to fly with me,
to delve life's true delights.

Does no one have the grit to seek
the deepest, truest word?
Is no one here to comfort me,
to heal *this* wounded bird?

Now healer must her own wounds treat,
her pinions to restore,
to rise once more to heights untold
like Phoenix bird of lore.

… We Ate Dog Biscuits!

My three clowns!

Tail-winder of a drive

Ever eat a dog biscuit?

You know, they're not half bad. They taste like a cross between melba toast and a very hard, no-salt pretzel. I also understand why those commercials say they clean a dog's teeth: there's a sand-like grit mixed right in (leaves you something to chew on for hours after, don'tcha know).

Now you're probably asking, "What in the world ever possessed you to eat a dog biscuit?"

O.K., I'll tell you.

It all started out innocently enough. My older daughter Sally and I were supposed to meet my younger daughter Katie (a senior at Bowling Green State University) and her "boyfriend" at the McDonalds restaurant in Clyde, Ohio (a good half-way point for us) at 6 p.m. on March 20.

Katie had been anxious for me to meet Aaron, and we'd managed to arrange our schedules so we could finally all get together that night.

You need to understand, my Katie vowed that she would never even *date* a guy, let alone get serious about one. So this is earth-shaking stuff, here. Besides, a week later I found out that Aaron had asked Katie to be his wife; hence, this meeting held no small significance (unbeknownst to me at the time).

However (as best-laid plans often have a wont to do), our evening did not turn out the way we had anticipated.

The roads were slightly wet when Sally and I left Ashland, but quite clear of snow. No problem. However the further northwest we traveled, the more the snowstorm intensified.

Now, I've driven through some pretty hair-raising conditions in my sullied and checkered past, but on this particular night we encountered roads that would have made a seasoned, snow-plow driver turn around and go home.

71

We confronted *HIGH* winds with three- and four-foot-deep snow drifts, which almost completely closed the four-lane highway on Route 20. And, as if that weren't treacherous enough, *underneath* those drifts lay two- to four-inch-thick, **very bumpy,** flood-water ice.

Vehicles lay scattered helter-skelter, everywhere we looked.

At 5:55 p.m.—five miles short of our destination—Sally and I sat in a several-mile-long, line-up of traffic (mostly semis), all sitting at a dead stop. Oc-casionally we would creep ahead a quarter-mile or so, then the whole line would stop again for another hour or longer at a time.

We did not reach our rendezvous point until nearly 10 p.m. Needless to say, we had to invent things to do in the cab of my little truck for those four, ensuing hours.

Now, I should mention that daughter Sally and I had one of those butt-your-heads-at-every-turn kind of relationships that typify many mother-daughter connections. She came out screaming and hadn't stopped since the moment she'd left home some years before.

By this time we *had* worked out a stand-back-and-give-each-other-plenty-of-space kind of relationship. But now, as she was back home on a brief interlude between musical tours, we found ourselves trapped together in the cab of a 1993 GMC Sonoma pickup.

What else could we do? We talked and told stories, we sang and re-lived our childhoods, we watched the road drift shut—and we found a new kind of kinship we both had been longing for.

> *We laughed a lot, we cried a little, and we ate dog biscuits.*

We laughed a lot, we cried a little, and we ate dog biscuits.

Hey, when you're hungry, you learn to improvise with what you have on hand: a Payday candy bar, two kinds of Tic-Tac's and a pocket-full of dog biscuits made up our entire inventory of edibles—except for one Chunky bar, which we decided to ration in case of a *real* emergency

Naturally, by the time we reached the McDonalds in Clyde, Katie and Aaron had long since given up on us and headed back to BGSU, which any sensible person would have done.

Any *really* sensible person would have stayed off the roads entirely—and only later did we learn that the authorities in a four-county area had declared a Stage III emergency that night.

(You must keep in mind we did leave home in passable weather conditions, on the first day of spring, no less.)

You'll be relieved to know that we made it back home in one piece around midnight, but I'm not sure my truck will ever be quite the same after our little "side trip" adventure through the flood plains of northern Ohio.

See, once, in an attempt to circumnavigate the traffic jam, we turned off on a back road, which turned into a more terrorizing experience than Cedar Point's Demon-Drop ride ever could!

Thanks to sand bags, snow shovel and a never-slow-down-through-a-snow-bank-or-you're-dead attitude, half an hour later we managed to make it back to State Route 20—at *exactly the same* place in the *same* line-up of semi's from which we had started.

(Our side-trip adventure didn't get us to Clyde any more quickly, as it turned out, but it did give us another tail-winder-of-a-story to tell.)

In the midst of what could have been a treacherous situation, Sally and I had a wonderful talk, and—at long last—we managed to make a connection that few mothers and daughters are ever lucky enough to realize.

With all the thousands of road-trip miles she already had under her belt (Sally toured for two years with the singing group *ReCreation*), she says that this is one trip she'll remember for a long, long time.

I will, too, cuz I'm still chewing on the grit from our dog-biscuit supper!

73

I flunked 'Grandma 101'

How could anyone possibly flunk "Grandma 101?"

Well now you can tell your neighbors you know someone who did. For you see, I've committed one of the biggest faux pas in grandmotherdom: I've failed to keep a photo album on my person, which documents every smile and "first" my brand new grandson achieves.

Wait—there's more: I haven't even put a *single picture* of that little angel-face into my purse, either!

"How could a grandmother NOT carry a photo of her very first grandchild?" you ask. Makes you wonder whether this so-called grandma has all her buttons, doesn't it?

I have to confess, I'm having trouble seeing myself as a grandmother. My *mother* is the one who's the grandmother—not me. She's also the one who pulled a photo album out of her purse when Aunt Marilyn asked to see a picture of new baby Daniel.

Now my mother's an old hand at this grandmothering stuff, but I'm still learning the ropes, here. Oh, I may have the age requirement down, all right, along with the gray hair and a well-stocked cookie jar. But the mind-set's all wrong.

What kind of grandmother would willingly walk backward off a cliff just to write a story about rappelling? Or brag about the distinction of being the first woman to spend a night in the new Holmes County Jail? (It was for another *story*, of course!) And what kind of grandmother looks forward to giving up a brand new house in order to go live in a 14-foot tipi?

You can see that learning traditional grandmother skills could present quite a challenge for this off-center grandma.

I did manage to get a little practice in over the holidays, though, when my kids traveled up from Tennessee to spend a few days here in Horsetail Hollow. Daniel slept through most of his first Christmas, but I made sure he knew that it was his obligation to wake his folks up bright and early Christmas morning.

> *Learning traditional grandmother skills presents quite a challenge for this off-center grandma!*

(I haven't forgotten those 4 a.m. Christmases after no more than two hours of sleep because we had to stay up until 2 a.m. putting together toys that came with the sticker "some assembly required.")

Don't worry, I gave Daniel's Mom and Dad plenty of time to sleep during the rest of their stay—but NOT on Christmas morning!

When six-week-old Daniel decided that he wanted to stay awake from 11 p.m. to 1 or 2 in morning's wee-hours, he and Grandma Marilee had a wonderful visit beside the sparkling Christmas tree lights, talking over "shoes and ships and sealing wax, cabbages and kings."

(We never did decide whether the sea is boiling hot, but we definitely agreed that some pigs do, indeed, have wings—since Daniel's fresh from those heavenly heights, his recollection of angel classifications far exceeds my own.)

And when he began to drift into that misty space between waking and sleeping, where little smiles flicker across a newborn's face from an angel's gentle kiss, I paid close attention. But I could never quite catch the echo of angel song nor observe a single feathery shadow.

My feet have plod this muddied earth far too long to verify such ethereal notions.

I'm sure that by the next time I see Daniel, he'll be more firmly bound to a waking life here. So my chance to catch angels in the wake of this grandchild has undoubtedly slipped away.

One *can* always hope for another such chance with the next grandchild! If that be the case, I'd better knuckle down and learn more about this grandmothering business so I'm ready.

Until another newborn comes along, Daniel and I will have to satisfy ourselves exploring the wonders of his new world together (on those rare occasions when I do get to see him, seeing as he lives so far away).

He can tell me what it feels like to look at everything from floor level, and maybe we can have a long discussion about the taste and texture of using dog biscuits as teething devices.

Starting the New Year off with a bang!
(And I do mean BANG!)

"INTRUDER ALERT!! INTRUDER ALERT! Yeeeeooowwww, Yeeeeooowwww!! Leave the premises immediately. You have violated a protected area... INTRUDER ALERT! INTRUDER ALERT!..."

Let me just start by saying that after a brush with armed police officers, I now know the alarm code at the Ashland location of *KD's Allegro Pizzeria*—headquarters for the KD's pizza shops (located in Ashland, Mansfield, and Wooster).

In case you didn't know it, I fell into another part-time job by default. It's a long story; the short version goes: my girlfriend made me do it. You see, her brother Eric owns all three pizza shops, and I got hooked into it when I volunteered to help her out "for a couple of weeks" with some first-of-the-year paperwork.

To date, I've been shuffling payroll and daily-reports for over two years, now. (Who'd have guessed a dyslexic Crackpot would turn into a numbers cruncher, of all things?!)

After two years of working at a place—trusted with computer passwords, signature stamps and my own, personal keys to the office, no less—you'd think that *someone* would have given me the code to the security system by now, wouldn't you?

Normally, I commence my office work somewhere between 7:30 and 8:30 a.m., after the pizza trucks have already loaded and taken off on their daily rounds to area factories.

By the time I arrive, the early morning manager has already disarmed the security alarm, so I can head right upstairs, unlock the main, office door and dive into my duties. No problems.

HOWEVER, during the recent holiday weeks of Christmas and New Year's, no one bothered to tell me that the catering trucks would NOT run—which meant that no manager would arrive early to disarm the security system.

Enter unsuspecting Crackpot with keys, but no alarm code.

The minute I opened the back door and heard the high-pitched whine, I knew I was in for a hair-raising ride.

"INTRUDER ALERT!! INTRUDER ALERT!!! Yeeoowww, Yeeeooww!! Leave the premises immediately. You have violated a protected area... INTRUDER ALERT! INTRUDER ALERT! Yeeeoowww, Yeeeoowww..."

"Good Grief, *now* what do I do?"

Have you ever tried to deal calmly with a situation while bells, whistles and ear-splitting alarms raise the hackles on the back of your neck? Geeze, the decibel level alone makes the ol' heart rate climb right up there (and I have to tell you, it doesn't take much these days to do that to this defective ticker).

Hells, bells, one of the main reasons I stuck with this job was because of the lack of stress involved—no deadlines, no personnel hassles, no set hours to punch a time clock. I could do my work in peace, and as long as I got my part of things done by payday, everyone was happy.

"O.K., girl, think. You need to call boss Eric and get the alarm code."

Without wasting time to search for the light switches (I never turn them on, because they're normally on when I arrive), I proceeded upstairs to the office, fumbling in the dark with the key until I managed to unlock the blasted door. (What with all that noise going on in the background, who could concentrate?)

Phones started ringing downstairs, and the phone started ringing upstairs. Since I never answer the downstairs phones (normally for pizza orders coming in—not my area) I let those ring.

How was I supposed to know *that's* the number the police always call if the alarm gets tripped?

By the time I dealt with the office phone upstairs (both lines—alarms still singing away) I finally got through to Eric.

At last, I had the code. *I could turn off that blasted noise!* But the minute I hit the top step on my way back downstairs to punch the code into the alarm's key-pad, I heard a creak on the bottom steps around the corner.

I knew I'd better make my presence known, post haste. "Hello!! I'm up here!"

The instant I hollered, I saw the gun jump in the hand of the police officer coming around onto the landing.

"What are you doing in here, lady?"

"I work here. No one told me the trucks wouldn't run today."

"What's your name, what do you do here? Why are the lights off downstairs?"

"Wait a minute, I can't hear a thing with that siren blaring. Let me disarm that thing before it drives me completely nuts! I just got the code from Eric."

Needless to say, the two officers scrutinized me at gunpoint, as I quieted the earsplitting noise. (Thank goodness the code worked!)

"O.K., now. What's your name, lady."

"MaryLee. That's my first name."

"What's the last name."

"Marilee. M-a-r-i-l-e-e."

> *"Is this supposed to be some kind of Christmas joke?"*

They gave each other a funny look. "Is this supposed to be some kind of Christmas joke?"

"No, that's my name. Really! MaryLee Marilee."

It took several minutes to convince the officers of my identity and answer their questions—apparently all to their satisfaction, since they did not end up hauling me off to the pokey.

The outcome of this little exercise in security is that we now know the Ashland Police Department will respond to the call with vigilance and haste.

I'm just mighty glad they did NOT send their police dog into the building first, before they entered with guns drawn, ready to deal with a deadly Crackpot.

Talk about starting the new year off with a bang!

I have to tell you my heart rate did not settle back to normal until close to noon. The whole thing gave me a bigger charge than three cups of high-test coffee and a mega portion of Ghirardelli® chocolate.

I now know the security code, thank goodness. And it's a mighty good thing. Cuz I'd much rather get my charge from the chocolate!

Snowball Beagle

Whoever heard of a dog who barks at snowballs?

Well, I have one who does. And for more than four hours straight, I had to listen to her bark at a big klunk of a snowball that rolled down off the roadway near my camper when a snowplow came through after our last big winter storm.

I showed her the darn thing was just a snowball, but she wouldn't believe me. She circled it from about three feet away, with fur raised and teeth bared, but try as I may, I couldn't convince her that it wasn't going to take off and chase her any minute.

Even after dispatching the snowball into the creek, she still stood and barked at the empty spot in the yard where that snowball had lain.

Now this ornery little bit of a dog has one of the most endearing personalities I've ever met in an animal, but she does test me to the limits of human endurance.

You see, she's a Beagle. And if you've ever made the acquaintance of a Beagle you know exactly what I mean. To say they're hardheaded is an understatement.

For starters, she's got definite ideas about her name. I call her Dinky. (As the runt of the litter, she couldn't muscle her way in among her fatter siblings to get much of the food.) But Dinky answers only to "Little Girl"—when she feels like it, that is.

Of course, if I have food in my hand, she'll come to anything I care to call her, but when I *want* her to come, you'd better believe she plays coy.

Like all dogs in the chewing stage (and for a Beagle, I believe that stage never ends), she'll shred most anything she can get her teeth into—leather, paper, tin cans, foil, rugs, shoes—you name it, she'll chew it up and make one whale of a mess in the process.

If that isn't enough, she's a thief and a scrounge, to boot. Since she discovered my neighbors' trash piles, it's hard telling what she's apt to drag into the yard next.

Last weekend, I looked out the window to see her racing in circles, pulling yards and yards of what appeared to be long streamers. She'd found an old cassette tape, chewed it apart and had a ball dragging that audio tape all over the yard making a huge pile of plastic spaghetti.

From what I've said so far, you might get the idea that I let her run loose, but the truth is, she's tied up all day, every day during the week while I'm at work. And because she spends so much time tethered, she's like a Tasmanian Devil when I let her loose in the evenings. She races in circles, tearing all over the place.

Dinky makes her rounds, saying "hello" to the neighbors, and to the neighbor's dogs, and to the other neighbor's llamas. Then she tries to mooch—or steal—anything edible she can find.

> *This is the only dog I know who actually wears her lips off by keeping her nose to the ground so much!*

The fact that I've already fed her (and she always races through her supper) is completely irrelevant, when it comes to that scrounge instinct. If she's not hungry at the moment, she'll simply bury it for later.

Now I know I'll never get the mileage out of my Dinky that Charles Schultz has gotten out of his Snoopy, but a Beagle is a Beagle is a Beagle when it comes to character.

Dinky definitely has character sticking out all over. This is the only dog I know who actually wears her lips off by keeping her nose to the ground so much.

Her hunting instinct just might have a bit of a kink in it, though, judging from the way she stalks a snowball!

Charlie Chipmunk and Debbie Dove

Did you know that acorns taste like macaroni and cheese? At least so says two-year-old Tessa Rose.

She assures me that while she's never tasted one herself, Charlie Chipmunk—who plays around her front yard every morning—eats acorns because he likes them. And since Tessa likes macaroni and cheese, how could acorns taste like anything else?

Grandmas dare not argue with that kind of logic.

I must admit, I've always enjoyed talking with preschoolers. They take in absolutely *everything* around them, stir it all up in those active little brains, and you never know how they're apt to put everything together until it comes tumbling out in the most serious of conversations—like Charlie Chipmunk and his macaroni-and-cheese tasting acorns.

Debbie Dove likes to come into Tessa's yard, too, by the way. But she eats birdseed and bugs. Tessa doesn't like to eat bugs. But she will eat worms, as long as they're the gummy-worm variety.

Mommies and daddies don't always have time to listen intently to such thoughtful discourse, since they're so busy doing what mommies and daddies have to do, in order to keep a growing household going strong.

But grandparents most assuredly do have the time. And this particular grandma takes her job quite seriously—along with keeping candy dishes full and plenty of cookies on hand, to boot.

Kids always check those things as soon as they walk through the door, you know.

I believe the biggest draw to visiting my little camper is roasting marshmallows and finding mini-candy bars in my little refrigerator.

That, and using the little potty. To a do-it-myself, two-year-old on the fresh side of potty training, finding a toilet she can climb onto without the aid of a stool or a grown-up comes as quite the novelty.

However four-year-old brother Daniel, who normally spends at least one night camping out with "Brrrraamma" during her visits, left Brrrraamma high and dry on this Tennessee trip. After setting up his camp bed and roasting one marshmallow, he announced that he thought he'd just better go back inside to sleep in his own bed this time.

Who knows—maybe he's heard too many scary camping stories. When you hit four, all sorts of scary things begin to creep around at night. And this grandma is fresh out of monster spray.

When my own kids hit that stage, I used to give the hair-spray can a squirt or two into dark closets and underneath beds to make the monsters disappear. But since I quit using hair spray years ago, once we left those poofy-doos of the 60s and 70s far behind us, nary a can of hair spray has darkened my toiletry shelf since.

Somehow a can of WD-40 doesn't quite do the trick.

Maybe next trip down Daniel will decide he's ready to camp with me again. Meanwhile, until Tessa discovers that she's missing out on something, this grandma will continue to camp with a ding-bat dog for her only company.

I can tell you, traveling with your own mother-in-law suite comes in mighty handy when the decibel level of two pre-schoolers reaches a pitch that no silence-loving grandma can manage to sustain for very long.

Having a little haven to which one can withdraw has distinct advantages.

It also helps to make a visit last longer, too. For I don't dare to leave before I learn more about Charlie Chipmunk and Debbie Dove!

Tin Can Technology

Did you ever set up a primitive communications system by stringing a set of old tin cans together? You remember the basic principle: stretch the string tight and holler like crazy into your can so the vibrations travel down the string into your partner's can.

You couldn't depend on that system to call up 9-1-1, but at least it kept a bunch of active kids busy, trying to see who could decipher the earth-shaking messages we'd send back and forth to one another from opposite sides of the barn.

I thought of that tin can technology, as I sat facing a tiny computer screen on the back of an airplane seat, when I had the opportunity to fly with USAir recently. Every seat in the plane came equipped with its own miniature computer monitor and combination control-panel/telephone.

Once airborne, passengers could make phone calls, play computer games or get the stock exchange report, buy gifts, send flowers and faxes, or cruise through schematics of all the country's major air terminals—right from the comfort of their own seats, as the plane streaked along, high above the clouds.

And by punching in the correct code (with proper credit card identification, of course), you could even receive phone calls right there in mid-air!

Quite a long stretch from those old tin cans, no?

With computer technology leaping forward almost daily, innovations like these passenger computers really shouldn't surprise me at all. I'm sure, to many people, they're already old hat. Yet every time I bump into some new gadget or gizmo, I never cease to be amazed.

I fumbled around with that telephone control stick for a while, and when I finally figured out how it worked, I played with

Computer phobia still has a way of paralyzing me at times.

my airplane-seat computer for quite some time. After all, I could hardly sit there and ignore the thing.

I didn't actually *do* anything with it, like make a phone call or order flowers or send a fax.

Call me a big chicken.

What if I'd keyed in the wrong code and broken into some top-security communications frequency, or cut off an important transmission in mid-fax, or interfered with air traffic control?

Computer phobia still has a way of paralyzing me at times, even though I think that I've gotten quite good at working with (and fighting with) our high-tech machinery at Graphic Pubs. (This stuff is great—as long as it works!)

I know modems and faxes, the Internet and cell phones are all here to stay, but I still sit in amazement when I meet something new like that airplane-seat computer. Who knows what astonishing innovations could possibly come next?

And to make them work, I bet you won't even need a can opener, either.

Telephone Tangle

"The green wire's connected to the red wire; (think 'Dem Bones here), *the red wire's connected to the black wire; the black wire's connected to the yellow wire, Ohhhhh help, I'm in way over my head!"*

Here I am, standing on a step ladder, with needle-nose pliers, electrician's tape, and a paring knife, trying to figure out this spaghetti-snarl of phone wire stuffed up in the corner of my basement ceiling.

It all started because of a call to phone repair service:

Wednesday morning a "Telephone Company Anonymous" repair truck pulled into the driveway and PhoneGuy proceeded to run a new cable for a computer/business phone, from the road to the primary phone box, already at work on the side of our house. Theoretically, all PhoneGuy had to do was hook up the second, computer line (already wired inside) to the new phone cable at that box.

He fixed everything up in short order, then left, before I even thought to have him check *both* phone lines.

The new number worked fine. No problem. However, all the other voice phones from our first line also worked on that same, new line. Somewhere both lines had been connected into one.

Sooooooo, I called the repair service 800-number.

"Hello? I need to get in touch with the service man who was just out here."

"Sorry, we have no way of knowing which service man was there, and even if we did, we have no way of getting in touch with him."

(This is a phone company, don't forget.)

"You mean to tell me you can't hook me up to the local service center?"

"Sorry, but we have no local dispatch numbers. All the service orders are placed by computer from the central office here in Wisconsin."

"You don't have anyone in Ohio who can help me find the man who was just here?"

"The best I can do is to put in another service order. Then we can have a repair man come back out there tomorrow, and you'll have to pay another service charge."

I'm sorry to say, that at this juncture I began to get a *teensy* bit upset, and I'm afraid I said a few things that no doubt came across sounding like a slur against the phone company.

After three more phone calls to Pam, Cindy and Dara in repair service (all of which ended in frustration) I gave up trying to get help from the phone company and began to trace down wires by myself.

To make a long story short, PhoneGuy had attached the new line to a 5" cord that ran only as far as the bottom of the outside box, where (after a previous useful life) it had been neatly cut off.

Then inside the house, I found that the computer line and voice line had been spliced together, where, some months ago during a remodeling project, some *other* PhoneGuy had hooked the whole shebang up to our primary number!

It's a good thing I managed to unsnarl everything and get both lines up and working at their respective phone jacks (dumb luck for sure), cuz I was getting ready to string up those tin cans!

A cracked pot, use glue, right?

Have you heard that nail polish remover will dissolve super glue? Well, I'm here to tell you that it did not—at least not in this particular instance.

You see, it all happened because of a pumpkin. With my kids coming for a holiday feast, and being the food purist that I am, I decided to bake my own pumpkins to use for pumpkin squares (a healthier alternative to pie, with no artery-clogging, shortening-laden crust).

Enter one tough little pumpkin and one BIG knife.

You guessed it. In the process of whacking my pumpkins in half for the oven, I slipped. Unfortunately my left thumb got the worst of the deal.

After raising three accident-prone children (who kept me on a first-name basis with the emergency-room staff for years), I have learned a thing or two about first aid.

Number one: staunch the flow of blood before you do anything.

Number two: look for detached body parts and put them on ice. Luckily, in this instance the end of my thumb still remained attached, flopping around, though it be.

Number three: after the bleeding has slowed or stopped, determine the necessity for stitches.

I have to say that I've saved many a trip to the emergency room by learning to fasten gaping wounds together with a butterfly bandage. However, it takes two good hands to accomplish that.

No problem. I've also learned that a touch of super glue to the severed parts can accomplish the same thing.

Hey, I'm told that doctors use that little trick on their own kids all the time to avoid stitches. If it's good enough for a doctor's kid, it's good enough for me.

Now, I've glued together many-a-crack in my winter-split fingers over the years without a single problem. But in the process of trying to affix this particular flapping appendage, the end of my super-glue tube stuck tight. Nothing.

Sooooooo, I retrieved a straight pin from the sewing table and proceeded to attempt the opening of said tube—no mean feat, while holding that tube in a hand with a bumb thumb.

We all know that when you poke a pin into something with inner pressure, whatever happens to be inside the container will undoubtedly come spouting out.

That pin released a big BLOOSH of super glue that splooshed all over the thumb and index finger of my *good* hand.

So there I stood—holding a straight pin with fingers super-glued together in one hand, and skin flopping on the thumb of the other.

Good grief, now what do I do??

Thankfully, I could still manage to dial a phone with the unaffected fingers. I called for assistance from my neighboring daughter. But I couldn't stop laughing long enough to explain my plight to the son-in-law who answered.

My brother, bless his heart, always says that the nut doesn't fall very far from the tree. In this particular case that statement applies to the in-laws, as well.

> My brother, bless his heart, always says that the nut doesn't fall very far from the tree.

I happen to have a second son-in-law who's particularly well acquainted with super glue, since his father was a glue salesman at one time and taught his boys how to get out of just such a fix. (Having three, ornery boys, you can imagine the fixes they got themselves into.)

Luckily for me, son-in-law #2 happened to be visiting at the time, so I had an expert come to my rescue.

Normally I wouldn't let anybody come at me with an X-acto® knife prepared to cut my fingers apart. However, the prospect of spending the next few days with my hand held in a perpetual "O.K." sign didn't thrill me a whole lot, either.

Suffice it to say that he did manage to emancipate his mother-in-law without leaving any bloody stubs.

I guess the next time I should listen to his three-year-old daughter who told me, "We're not supposed to put glue on our fingers, Grandma!"

Phantom!

*PAUMM*M—*PA*, PA*, Pa, Pa,* pa, pummm—pa, Pa, PA*, PA-PAUMMM*!! (Think huge, pipe-organ, minor chords here, with full orchestral backup that rattles your teeth and raises goose bumps down your neck.)

Granted, it loses something when you try to translate a musical effect into the written word, but if you've ever heard any music from Andrew Lloyd Webber's *Phantom of the Opera,* you know what I'm striving for here.

My daughter, Katie, had longed to see *Phantom* for years—especially since sister Sally had already seen it twice. (And according to Katie, "*No* one ought to be allowed to see *Phantom* twice, until *everyone* gets to see it once!")

Sooooooo, to celebrate my youngest daughter's 21st birthday, I took Katie to see *Phantom of the Opera* at the Pantages Theatre in Toronto.

Both of us still reel from the experience. To say it overwhelmed is an understatement.

Never have I seen such innovative staging or opulent costuming, not to mention music that knocks your socks off. Even if you're not an "opera" fan, I guarantee you won't find this production boring. I didn't see a dry eye in the place.

The setting alone gives an unbelievable backdrop to the whole *Phantom* experience. The restored Pantages Theatre drips with gold leaf and rich, burgundy brocades throughout.

When we took our seats (after sitting 6½ hours on the trip up to Toronto), I must admit, that judging by the theatre's grand ambiance up to that point, the stage disappointed me. Draped in yards of dark swathing, it looked rather gloomy.

But as lights dimmed and the orchestra struck its first minor chords, an air of anticipation permeated the whole theatre—gloomy-looking or not.

The play itself opens as an auctioneer puts theatre props and memorabilia on the auction block in a dilapidated old opera house with faded backdrops sagging and broken props strewn across the stage. After a few items sell to the highest bidders, he moves on to the next, shrouded item up for bid—an item which had played a large part in that ancient theatre's legends—a chandelier.

Suddenly the dusty cover pulls away, laser lights bounce back and forth through the whole theatre, and, as the chandelier bursts into light, it swoops to the ceiling, and all the gloomy swaddling disappears from the stage to reveal a grandiose opera company at the height of its magnificent, golden heyday.

Talk about a great hook!

After such an intro, I didn't know how the pro-

> Live theater—nothing quite matches the interplay of real people emoting on stage to real people reacting in the audience. You can't beat it.

duction could possibly get any better. Suffice it to say that in all my years of theatre-going, nothing I've seen can top this production of *Phantom*.

(And I've seen my share of theatrical productions—just ask my brother, whom I dragged to any number of "experimental" plays during my college years!)

I highly recommend attending live theater, by the way. Nothing quite matches the interplay of *real* people emoting on stage to *real* people reacting in the audience. You can't beat it.

Oh, did you want me to tell you the rest of the *Phantom* story? If I did that, it would spoil the whole ending for you, and what good is any story without a surprise ending to take your breath away?

I will tell you this much: the *Phantom* begins with a wallop and ends in a whisper; so much more is packed in between, I couldn't begin to tell the whole story in this limited space. Webber definitely outdid himself with this one.

Tickets for the production did cost dearly, and the theatre was booked *far* in advance, but if you *ever* get the chance to see

Andrew Lloyd Webber's *Phantom Of The Opera,* by all means, *do it!* I'd gladly miss dinners for another month just to see it again!

By the way, if you hear the minor strains of *Phantom* blaring from a little red pickup truck as it goes through town, it's just me. (And since I lost all those clear, operatic soprano tones long ago, I'll try to control myself when I sing along.)

"The Phaaaantom of the Opera is there, inside my mind!"

The adventures of Carlos, the misguided Tree Toad

Who goes to Florida in the summer heat?

Enter Thelma and Louise—although for this trip, Thelma and I decided to change our aliases to Penny the sultry and Ginger the ditz. (You can't have too many alter egos, as far as we're concerned.)

Yes, we really did head to Florida—Fort Myers, in fact—on a mission to bring back my 82-year-old mother-in-law for a month-long visit up north. (Although she and I haven't been official relatives for 20 years, we've always claimed one another.)

As you can imagine, Florida's BLISTERING this time of year. We had four days to sight-see and relax before heading back to Ohio, which included a jaunt to the beach, as well as a day of browsing the swanky boutiques of Naples.

Our last day, however, proved to be the most eventful of the lot. Now enters Carlos, the misguided tree toad.

As we lounged the late afternoon of our last day away, we decided to make a trip up to the compound's pool for a little dip before dinner. Getting changed into our suits, Penny used the bathroom first, and upon completion of her task, she discovered that something new had been added—a living, brownish-green, toad-like blob stuck to the back of the toilet seat.

Her screaming and hysteria alerted me to the fact that something was definitely amiss. Flying out of the bathroom half-clad, she dragged our hostess (alias Trixie) and me, Ginger, back to see the uninvited amphibian.

There he was, sticking with those little suction-cup toes to the back of the seat.

"I SAT right there, *against* him! Ewwww! Ewwwww! *Ewwwwwwww!*"

Being the more level-headed of the lot, I attempted to trap him in a hand towel, but the little bugger was just too quick.

"I told you it wouldn't work," said Trixie. "I've tried that before. You can't flush 'em. They won't go down."

Amid more screaming (this time from more than one of us), Carlos ended up in the drink.

So I slammed the lid and flushed.

No good. Those sticky toes held on for dear life.

"I told you it wouldn't work," said Trixie. "I've tried that before. You can't flush 'em. They won't go down."

"O.K.," says I. "Shut the lid and close the door. We're going swimming. Maybe he'll make his escape while we're gone."

Up at the pool, we described our dilemma to a savvy-looking gentleman also enjoying the facilities.

"Use those things you pick up hot dogs with. That's what I do," says he.

"You mean tongs?" asks Penny.

"Yup. Just don't squeeze 'em too tight."

"Ewwww! Ewwwww! *Ewwwwwwwwww!*"

After our swim, we returned and carefully scoped out the bathroom. Sure enough, Carlos still clung to the side of the commode.

I attempted to pin him down with the tongs, while Penny held a bath towel at the ready and Trixie held the door.

Boy, are those toads ever slippery devils. We had no luck with the tongs. After two tries, amid lots more screaming all around, we gave up on that idea. Penny headed for a strainer.

But a rounded strainer against a rounded bowl does not a flat/smooth surface make against which to capture a toad.

Amid the stirring and flailing around with that strainer, Carlos got out of the bowl, behind the commode, onto the mirror, then over to the shower wall.

"CATCH HIM!!!"

Whappo! Penny managed to trap him in a bath towel against the glass, shower door.

"Get outta my way, I'm comin' through!" She barreled out the bathroom door, through the bedroom, through the lanai, and out onto the lawn, where she threw down the towel and proceeded to scream some more, just for good measure.

Was he really in that towel?

We were all afraid to look.

"O.K., I'll look," says Penny with a brave front. She slowly unfolded the towel, and there, sitting on the grass is Carlos.

"He's free! Carlos is FREE!" (And still in one piece, which is the more amazing feat of the entire afternoon's shenanigans.)

Farewell Carlos. Have a good life—and don't come back in here again!

We toasted Carlos with well-deserved afternoon cocktails, and laughed our bellies sore at the escapade.

You can be sure that from now on, however, we're *always* gonna look before we sit!

Giving Thanks in all things

Haul out the squirty whipped-cream can. It's Thanksgiving—and this year we definitely need the comic relief!

Humor from Thanksgiving? What could you possibly find funny about offering thanks for a world filled with bombing raids, fiscal uncertainty, and the continued threats of terror, you ask?

O.K., since you asked, I'll tell you. With people pulling closer to loved ones in times of confusion and unrest, sitting down to a Thanksgiving feast with the family could open the door to just about anything—especially if you're part of a quirky clan like mine.

When you pull out a can of whipped cream, you never know what's liable to happen!

I can tell you from experience, if ever a time existed when we needed the crazy release of off-the-wall humor (or perhaps *on* the wall, if Uncle John gets hold of that can) it certainly is now.

But whipping cream?

It's a long story, but the nut-shell version goes something like this:

One holiday season some twenty-plus years ago, a Crackpot who shall remain nameless faced a personal crisis of life-altering proportion. (When your world falls apart, it takes some doing to fit the pieces back together again; it definitely does not get repaired overnight.)

As I sat at the traditional clan gathering, after having been released from the protective environment of a hospital that very day, the family all walked on pins and needles, not sure how to handle the shattered soul, cowering in their midst.

Now I need to preface this story with a little side-story to help explain what happened next. You see, some months earlier on a family fishing trip, I had endeared myself to my baby brother by smacking him in the face with a gooey chocolate pie.

That pie had spent the entire day in a sun-heated car while we fished for king salmon on Lake Michigan. By the time we pulled back into shore at dusk, the pie was definitely way beyond human consumption.

So rather than just pitch the thing in the trash, I did what any creative, resourceful person would do—I threw it at my brother!

What can I say? When I love someone, sometimes I have an unconventional way of showing it.

Now returning to aforementioned holiday gathering, where the entire family had been thoroughly instructed not to say or do *anything* that could possibly upset MaryLee.

(Needless to say, you could literally cut the tension in the room with a butter knife.)

Enter ornery little brother intent on retribution, hiding something behind his back.

Before anyone could say, "Please pass the pumpkin pie," I found myself plastered in whipped cream.

> *In his own, resourceful way, my brother demonstrated that regardless of what might be totally wrong in my life, his love would always be there to see me through the tough times.*

In his own, resourceful way, my brother demonstrated that regardless of what might be totally wrong in my life, his love would always be there to see me through the tough times.

With one, off-the-wall action, he not only conveyed his undying devotion to a Crackpot sister needing encouragement, he also managed to break the tension and return our family to relative normalcy (even though we all know that normal is only a setting on the clothes dryer).

My only regret from that momentous occasion, is that no one had a camera at the ready to memorialize the look of sheer horror on my mother's face at the instant she saw that whipped-cream pie poised to smack me in the schnoz.

Absolutely priceless!

Suffice it to say, that I gave my brother the biggest whipped-cream hug you can imagine.

From that day to this, you never know what's liable to happen at one of our family gatherings—or what's apt to fly.

At any Thanksgiving time, giving thanks for the good things in life comes easy. But when it feels as if the world is falling apart around us, offering gratitude for tough situations presents a greater challenge.

This year, we're called to do just that—say, "Thanks, Lord," in spite of all the craziness afoot.

So, if you're having trouble coming up with a reason to feel thankful, take my advice and haul out a can of whipped cream.

At least you can have a little fun—even if you do have to clean up the mess!

The crazy days of construction
(Think 12 days of Christmas)

On the first day of October construction gave to me, a big mud hole in the side yard.

On the same day of construction this project gave to me, two dozers working, one track-hoe digging, and a bigger mud hole in the back yard.

This building project brought to us more challenge than we knew—three neighbors talking, two backhoes working, one mobile-home buried, and a big mud hole in the neighbor's yard.

The next day of construction, this project gave to me, four pickups parking (tearing up the yard), three neighbors laughing, two trailers jockeying (tearing up the yard), two dozers working —to move two cement trucks buried, one Bobcat scurrying (to empty aforementioned cement trucks), *and a huge mud hole in the front yard!*

Who knows what this construction site will bring to us today? Countless pickups parking, busy track-hoes digging, *three neighbors shaking their heads!* Heaven only know how many dozers it will take to deliver Grant and Sally's new home (and extract it from the mud holes all over this place as they install it upon 45, count 'em, 45 new, cement piers!)

(End musical interlude!!)

In case you haven't guessed by now, we have big doin's going on here in Horsetail Hollow. The process of moving out my daughter and son-in-law's out-grown, mobile home and installing a new, double-wide, modular in its place has turned this entire neighborhood upside down—quite literally, I might add.

We now have mud holes front, back, and beside our home here in RoeLee Manor, not to mention huge ruts across the neighbor's yard where the old trailer got stuck not once, but twice in the process of moving it out.

But guess what? Once the new home is delivered and set firmly on its prepared site, the digging will need to start all over again, as our excavation expert installs a septic system for Grant and Sally's "new digs."

Meanwhile, Grant, Sally, two babies, and all their worldly possessions have squeezed into RoeLee Manor with Aunt Lou and me, to hole-up for the duration of this project.

> *When you have such a hilarious sideshow going on out there in the front yard, who can help but laugh?*

To say we're laughing a lot is an understatement. We figure laughing beats crying any day. Besides, when you have such a hilarious sideshow going on out there in the front yard, who can help but laugh?

Two—count 'em, two—cement trucks stuck in the front yard yesterday, as they delivered their goopy contents to form piers for this new home's foundation.

As fate (and the foresight of our expert digger, Mr. Bob) would have it, we had two bulldozers on site, available for the necessary extraction work.

(That was definitely a good thing, I can tell you.)

Who knows what great hilarity the rest of this week has in store, until we see a new house sitting firmly on its foundation.

I'll be sure to keep you posted.

In the meantime, we may as well enjoy all that mud out there, cuz Lord knows we're going to see a lot more of it before this project comes to an end.

Hey, anybody up for mud wrestling?

Are you a member of the Whoopie Club?

No, I'm not talking about a bunch of pimple-faced teens who get their jollies by sneaking a Whoopie cushion underneath Great-aunt Martha or Uncle Herbert.

I'm talking about those of us who drive a trusty, rusty vehicle that made its debut before the first George Bush occupied the White House—like the little Pontiac 6000 station wagon I've been driving for the past year.

I call him "Eric the Red" (the car, not George Bush).

So far, while keeping this Whoopie on the road, I have not crossed that line of demarcation which shows my monetary outgo tipping the scales more toward the "parts and labor" side, rather than the side marked "new car payment and higher insurance."

But I have to admit, constant trips to the repair garage are beginning to get tedious...

"Would you describe the noise it's making, Ma'am?"

"Well, it sounds a little bit like an airplane engine getting ready for take-off, only not quite so loud."

"How does it act on the road?"

If I *ease* the accelerator down after a stop or up a hill, Eric the Red does fine. But if I step on the gas as I normally would, he does this herkey-jerkey kind of sputter, then gives a backfire or two before he coughs his way up to speed.

"Sounds like a fuel-pump problem, to me," says a mechanic.

"Sounds like a timing chain, if you ask me," says another.

"How much $$ are you guys talking here," ask I (as if I really want to know.)

"You don't want to know," say both together.

Which brings me to my present dilemma: Do I add yet another quirk to Eric's already growing list of character flaws and continue to drive him "as is," or do I haul him to the junk yard to sell for parts?

I already have to make sure his rpm's don't drop below 1000, otherwise he stalls out. The cruise control never has worked since I acquired him about a year ago. But who really needs cruise control on the rolling hills of Amish and Mohican country, anyway?

I seldom lock Eric, because from the outside, I can only UN-lock the driver's side door, and then only if I insert the key just right, since my #1 Grandson with the key fetish bent the only key I have when he jammed the lock on the passenger-side door (which makes that key impossible to duplicate.)

Then there's his radio (the car's, not the grandson's). Sometimes it works; sometimes it won't work. And when it does decide to play, you never really know what station you have, because there's no digital read-out—except sometimes.

You see, Eric was a state-of-the-art car in his heyday—computerized everything, superwammedon digital readouts for every function, no dials or dummy-lights here. Of course, that means now, in his waning years, you never know for sure if those choppy-lined read-outs give anywhere near accurate readings—which makes every trip an adventure.

I did discover that even though his windshield-wiper lever has broken off of the turn-signal switch, Eric still has this teensy tail of a piece of plastic that will activate the windshield washer, if I pinch and twist it with just the right amount of pressure. So I no longer need to hold a squeeze bottle out the window to wash away snow slush or road schmutz.

The wipers do work, of course, but I have to give the driver's side arm a hearty punch at its base every now and then, just to make sure it doesn't come off in mid-wipe.

Did I mention Eric's air conditioning? I do have air, but not the traditional, mechanical variety. Mine's 4/60 air—four windows down at 60 mph, guaranteed to blow away sweat even in the heat of Southern Florida. (Last fall Eric actually got me down there—and back!)

I suppose you're wondering, "why would anyone in her right mind drive such a vehicle?"

> *4/60 air—four windows down at 60 mph, guaranteed to blow away sweat even in the heat of Southern Florida.*

It's simple: I like Eric the Red. He has character—a little like his owner (although I've never known anyone to own a vehicle by the way; truly they own us).

Besides, whoever claimed this Crackpot was ever in her right mind?

So, if you happen to find yourself stuck in a line of traffic, creeping along at 35 mph. up one of the long hills on SR 39 between Loudonville and Millersburg, do not despair. As soon as Eric the Red makes it to the top, we'll pull over so all you speed demons can pass.

I imagine this old Whoopie will make it to town 'long about the time all those buggies do!

Let 'em Eat Cake

Marie Antoinette had nothing on my Sal when it comes to dishing it out—cake, that is.

Now at any wedding, one expects to see a little cake spread around on the respective bride and groom's faces, but at my daughter Sally's wedding, things hardly progressed in the "expected" manner at any given turn—cake-eating included.

Perhaps I should preface this whole column by telling you that I happen to have clowns for kids. And with three children like that, you can hardly expect their chosen mates to be any less the comedians, either.

Let me hasten to say, that the wedding ceremony itself couldn't help but move everyone in the congregation. Seldom does one hear soloists who really can *SING* at a wedding, nor does one find any bride or groom who can repeat their vows from memory without coming to tears or breaking eye contact during the entire thing.

J. Grant and Sally not only wrote and recited their own vows, Grant composed an entire song for Sally and sang it to her, complete with orchestral backup. (They carried it all off without a hitch [no pun intended], but don't forget, these two *are* seasoned performers.)

Of course, after such an emotionally charged interval, any good performer knows the need for a moment of comic relief. But—unbeknownst to Sally or Grant—when the minister (Uncle Art) asked for the ring, the ring-bearer held up an empty pillow, then looked beseechingly at the best man, who searched all his pockets in vein.

The best man looked to the groomsman beside him, who also searched his pockets, then he, in turn, looked to the next man in line. The same scenario proceeded down the entire line of seven groomsmen and all their empty pockets hanging out, until the last one produced the long-awaited wedding ring. By the time all seven passed the ring back up to the minister, the entire congregation was in stitches.

From that point on, although serious moments in the ceremony did ensue, one never quite took for granted that the wedding and reception would progress in any "normal" context.

With the reception's theme, "Have Fun and Be Creative," how could we expect the conventional from this bunch?

Before I say more, I must pause to give special thanks to Aunt Donna Johnston, who coordinated the entire wedding day and kept things running smoothly (despite several unexpected turns). Thanks, Donna and brother Jim, for all your work in planning, setting up and cleaning up after the fact.

This Crackpot pooped out on the clean-up work, since I could hardly stand up by the end of the reception, as I had stayed up the whole night before the wedding re-making an entire bride's maid's dress. (I learned a very important lesson: never believe measurements *someone else* has taken. And ALWAYS allow extra fabric to let out, so you don't have to cut out a whole new gown at the last minute!)

The whole wedding party ended up looking wonderful in their hand-beaded, tuxedoed glory, and they all had a blast at the reception—as did everyone in attendance.

From holding up score cards for each kiss (a'la Olympics tradition) to kidnapping the groom and charging admission to see him in bell-trimmed boxer shorts, these kids took the "Be Creative" dictate to heart.

And when it came to the cake, even a Mickey-Mouse bib for the groom and Minnie-Mouse bib for the bride didn't prepare folks for what came next.

Sally carefully cut the cake. She deliberately handed J. Grant one piece, then she took hers, pausing only a moment before they each shoved their respective pieces—not in each other's faces—but in the faces of the best man (Jim's brother Jeff) and maid of honor (Sally's sister Katie) standing beside them!

> *Even a Mickey-Mouse bib for the groom and Minnie-Mouse bib for the bride didn't prepare folks for what came next.*

Now we all wait with baited breath to see what retaliation Katie has cooked up for her sister. For you see, now we get to do the whole wedding thing all over again for Katie and Aaron three weeks hence, on Aug. 31!

Wish me luck—after one emotionally-charged wedding already this month, I don't know if the Kleenex® company is up to supplying me with enough tissues for another nuptial event so quickly!

This time, at least, the attendants' dresses are of a style that's much easier to fit. And maybe (if I'm lucky) after a summer of sewing 22 dresses (two of which were bridal gowns with more than 2500 hours of beaded and sequined work invested) the mother of the bride will have time to make a dress for herself and not have to wear her favorite one from Goodwill—yet again!

The Bride wore tennis shoes

My Katie did it—she really wore tennis shoes for her wedding ceremony. Now we're not talking ordinary tennis shoes here, mind you, but all bedecked with lace, beads and sparkly doodads. Honest-to-goodness tennis shoes they were, nonetheless.

She and Aaron Zink, her new husband, also wore swim goggles through the bird-seed barrage outside the church, and they made their grand entrance into the reception hall wearing Groucho glasses, complete with noses and mustaches!

An ordinary couple these two definitely are not.

Not only did the congregation, gathered to witness this knot-tying, have a lot of fun, they also got a little taste of the combined strength that holds Katie Conrad and Aaron Zink together.

You see, these two made a joint decision not to kiss before their wedding day. I know, as far-fetched as that may sound in this day and age, they really did stick to that commitment (even though it nearly killed Aaron, especially!).

Most of their college friends knew of their unusual decision, but only after the minister shared that information with the congregation (amid many blank stares and head shaking) did most of the extended family and friends learn the significance of what the coming words, "you may now kiss your bride," would really mean!

When that moment finally did arrive, a hush fell over the entire sanctuary as Aaron just stood there, looking at Katie, not making a move.

(Before I tell you what happened next, I need to insert a little information here. When Katie's sister Sally wed just three weeks earlier, Sal and her husband Jim hit about an 11 on the kiss-o-meter scale of 1-10. Minister Uncle Art said it beat any he'd ever seen before; he bet Katie 50 cents that she couldn't out-do her sister.)

"You may now kiss your bride."

After that pregnant pause, Aaron grabbed Katie and proceeded to knock the kiss meter completely off the scale. The place exploded in applause, laughter and acorn whistles (I always carry an acorn lid for just such an occasion.)

When Katie walked back down the aisle as Mrs. Aaron Zink, Uncle Art reached over and handed her a dollar bill!

Now everyone waited with baited breath to see what might happen at the reception. We all knew Katie had some kind of payback cooked up for Sally. (At Sal's wedding, as you recall, Katie ended up wearing the wedding cake instead of her sister the bride.)

Friends and relatives had a great time, eating, visiting and writing crayon-messages to the bride and groom on the table paper. But just before cake-cutting time arrived, about a dozen baseball-bat-wielding, uninvited guests—decked out in pinstriped, zute-suits and mafia hats—crashed the party.

In a gravelly voice, the Godfather of "Da Family" informed the wedding party of his displeasure at being "left out" of the guest list, and he proceeded to grill the Conradios and Zinkolas to see if they "checked out" as suitable members to add to "Da Family."

Then he started talking about a certain matter of *"retribution"* that concerned Katie and her sister. During this little diversion, three of the "hit men" had made their way to the head table and flanked Sally so she couldn't run.

When they grabbed her and held her tight, Katie pulled a can of whipped cream from beneath her dress, then she took a plate, sprayed it full of that foamy stuff, and smooshed it into her sister's face.

Payback time!

110

Sally gave Kate a huge whipped-cream hug.

I think most everyone went home that night smiling, remembering the day's many moments of pure joy and celebration.

But I have to be honest with you—it was not all fun for me. I had trouble letting go of this particular chick. Sally has always been my independent bird, but Katie's my baby. And as she flew the coop for good, I knew my nest was finally empty.

This last wedding signaled a huge shift for me. Now all my kids have new priorities, and they each belong to someone else. My care-taking days have finished. (I've always maintained that when a mother does her job well, she works herself right out of a job!)

Now I look forward to the next stage—spoiling grand-children. And I can't wait to give them acorn-whistle lessons!

Riddles of the Road

If you want to travel any farther than you can hoof it, we need wheels—there's no way around it.

And if you commute your miles to work in the double-digits every day, it pretty well locks you into depending on some kind of wheels to get there in time to punch the time-clock.

Enter the automobile—or in my case, small pickup truck. I've tried to fight it, but I'm a truck person through and through. However after my latest adventure with my daughter's car, I am considering giving up motorized vehicles altogether and trading my truck in on a good mountain bike! Or a donkey. Anyone got a nice little donkey?

You see, my daughter's car needed mechanical help, and since my son is a terrific mechanic, he volunteered to work on the car for her. Only one problem: he's in Tennessee, and she's in Loudonville.

Guess who got drafted to drive the car down there? *"You'll get to spend a few days with your grandson while Jim works on the car, Mom."* I write this from my temporary quarters in the "mother-in-law suite" in Hampton, Tennessee.

You'll be happy to know that I made it down before the timing-belt broke through, which would have stopped the car dead in its tracks and ruined the engine completely, I'm told. *(Good thing nobody told me that BEFORE I got in the car to drive the nine hours it takes to get here!)*

The bad news is, that when Jim took off the timing belt (practically crumbled in his hands) he discovered that the water pump needed replacing, along with all the hoses and belts, and the distributor cap… and the radiator… and the wheel bearings… and the universal joint and the…

Well, I won't bore you with the rest, but it looks as if I'll get the chance to be well acquainted with the auto-parts dealers in this Tri-City area of Tennessee, as well as with my grandson.

Now if you've racked up any windshield-time at all, I'm sure you've also had your share of highway adventures. I'd be willing to bet my greasy bucket full of blown gaskets, here, that you have mechanical-failure horror stories to tell, too.

So after many-a-highway misadventure, I've developed this list of "Riddles for the Road." (By the way, these riddles have no answers, so if you DO come up with any, by all means please enlighten me!)

1) Why is it that when your car stops cold as you're driving along, it always stops:

a) in the middle of a crowded intersection;

b) on the upgrade of a steep hill where the on-coming traffic cannot see you;

c) in the apex of a bad curve with no room at all to get off the road, or

d) on the interstate with no exits for miles in either direction?

2) Why is it if you run out of gas, you:

a) don't have a gas can along; or

b) if you *do* have one, it's empty, too?

3) Why is it that when your battery goes dead (because the kids left the dome lights on all night after the basketball game), the jumper cables are in the "beater car"—which the kids took to school and which ALWAYS runs?

4) Why is it that when you have a flat tire, no one stops to help until you have the last lug nut tightened (if anyone even bothers to stop at all)?

5) Why is it that when you take your car to a mechanic, it'll never make the same noise in the repair shop that it does on the road? Cars (like kids) make a liar out of you every time.

I do have to say that this car of my daughter's fooled me completely. It didn't make a single rattle or squeal or knock or ping the whole way down here—smooth sailing all the way down US 23, over the Virginia mountains—even through the "blasting zone."

But now it looks as if I'll be down here for a while: you see, the front axle is over in that corner of the garage, the air cleaner and water pump are sitting in that other corner, the wheels are over there, and I won't even mention brakes, or oil pump or the struts or...

(In case I don't get back to Ohio right away, would someone save a few of the prettiest fall leaves for me?)

Which wrench you say?

"Hand me that 17 millimeter socket down there, would you, Mom?" says my mechanically minded son, who's been working on his sister's car for the past week-and-half.

I look at a whole pile of tools lying next to the pieces he's already torn out of that little Volkswagen Jetta and grab one that looks like a wrench to me.

"This one?"

"No, that's a half-inch extension. I need a metric socket that fits on top. It looks a little bit like this one."

I see a greasy hand reach out from under the car holding a stubby-looking piece of metal that resembles a cup.

"Maybe I'd better look over there by that other pile of parts."

I take a flashlight (it's pushing midnight here) and pick my way through grease-smeared metal pieces-parts till I find a tool that comes close to matching.

"This it?"

"Close. You're five millimeters off. It should be next to that wheel over there."

Third time's a charm, right? So I hand him one more tool and hope for the best.

"Thanks, Mom. Now, reach under here and hold the end of this wrench steady while I get the timing belt set in the right position."

"What happens if I let it slip?"

"We ruin it and you make another trip to the parts store."

(Just so you know what's going on, my daughter-in-law and I have already made 10 trips to at least seven different auto-parts stores here in the Tri-Cities area of eastern Tennessee on our quest to track down foreign parts for this little lemon of a car.)

115

"You really want ME to hold this thing tight?!"

"Relax, Mom. You can do it."

"O.K. I'll give it a shot. You know I'm always up for adventure."

Fact is, the whole adventure started when I agreed to drive my daughter and her husband's little car down to Tennessee where my son (the airplane mechanic) could "fix it for them." They figured I be back home in a week.

Here we are, two weeks later (and many hundreds of dollars' worth of parts poorer) and Jimbo's still burning the midnight oil after his "day job" at Moody Aviation, trying to get this little car back together again.

I can't say that I'm sorry to be stuck down here in Tennessee with my little grandbaby Daniel. During these two weeks I've had the opportunity to watch him change from a crab-crawling babe to a top-heavy toddler paddling all over the house on two tiny feet.

At his current pace, I predict he'll be running by next week—then nothing in the house will be safe!

In some ways this has been a bitter-sweet kind of visit, for as I watch little Daniel discover his world, memories of my own son wash over me. I see flashes of his daddy in Daniel's actions and manner (as when he works for 20 minutes trying to maneuver the adult-sized broom around the kitchen in an attempt to sweep like Mama—such concentration for one so small!)

I remember another boy, just as focused and intent upon mastering things far beyond his childhood abilities, and I feel an empty longing to hold my own babies again.

But that time fades far into the distant past.

Funny, I don't feel all that much older. It seems only yesterday I was the one changing diapers, wiping runny noses, and kissing little boo-boos to make the hurts go away.

But now, as I watch Daniel toddle around—falling on his caboose, getting up, then falling down again—I marvel at the perseverance of the human spirit and thank all that's holy for the chance to have seen my children grow and prosper and procreate.

The whole cycle begins once again.

> *I marvel at the perseverance of the human spirit and thank all that's holy for the chance to have seen my children grow and prosper and procreate.*

"Hey, Mom... Mom?"

"Hmmmm?"

"Hand me that wrench you're holding, would you," he says, extending a greasy hand.

"Sure."

"Say, how come this thing's all wet?"

I take a deep breath and blow my nose. "Have I told you lately how proud I am of you, Jimbo?"

"You may not feel that way when I tell you what I just broke."

"Another trip to the parts store?"

"Another trip to the parts store."

Half a Century and still learning!

Break out the fire extinguishers before this cake goes up in flames!

Can you believe it? Fifty candles for this Crackpot? But I thought I turned 25 just a couple years ago. What happened? How did we come this close to the century's flip-page already?

Fess up—who's the wise-guy who pushed that giant fast-forward button?

Why "back when I was a girl, some 40+ years ago... I can remember... " (Don't you just hate it when people start a boring reminiscence that way?)

But I *can* remember that little girl. And she thought that by the time we got this close to the year 2000, she'd be an old bag at 50 years old! Who'd have guessed she could have been so grievously misled?

Think about it: to a kid, 50 *is* old. But now that I've actually arrived at this place in time, I look back and wonder how in blazes I got so far already when I just started on this earthly sojourn only last week.

(I'll tell you a secret: it *was* only last week. This whole "time" thing—a figment of our imaginations. Doesn't exist! Just ask Einstein, he knew.)

Know something else pretty remarkable? This year not only do I cross over the half-century mark, but my mother turns 75, my youngest daughter turns 25, and she's about to give birth to another generation to boot. So in another 25 years, we'll have a whole century covered!

I want to tell you a little story, but I must preface it with this: my mother has always loved the hymn, *Shall we gather at the river?* You know the song:

"Shall we gather at the river, where bright angel feet have trod; with its crystal tide forever flowing by the throne of God..."

I have a deep memory that goes way back (lots more than 50 years) to before the time I was even born.

Now let me qualify this by saying that if you prefer to take my recollection as the rantings of a crazy woman, that's fine; I'll accept that appellation with pride. If you choose to see it as a dream, so be it. But to the very core of my being I know that it's absolutely true.

I can remember looking down at a river from a very high, dark place, watching the currents ebb and flow, and seeing points of light at various spots within that current. At some places those lights appeared closer together than at others. But I can remember feeling particularly drawn to a specific collection of lights. And the more I focused upon those lights, the closer I felt to them.

Eventually I felt such a strong pull, that I flew toward those lights and landed in their very midst.

Those points of light were the souls I knew and loved, after they had taken on physical form and had been temporarily anchored in that flowing river's crystal tide—in physical existence, if you please.

We are those lights—*frozen* lights.

> **We are those lights — frozen lights**

Now I won't go into the quantum physics of the whole thing, but suffice it to say that Einstein and his cronies pushed over the domino that began the tumble down that whole line of thought.

Each one of us *is* a frozen point of light, you see, living in that crystal river at this very moment. And the bright angel-feet tread with us here, every day, guiding us through the ebb and flow—through the rapids and white-water—of our individual existences.

They're protecting us, helping us to help one another, and keeping us on our individual paths of learning until we come to that place where our lights will once again be set free.

All the while, this river keeps flowing by the throne of grace, through every hour of every day of our physical lives—temporarily trapped in this river of time—and far, far beyond.

All right, all right. I see you over there. Yes you—the one in the white coat. That's a straightjacket you're holding. I know it is.

(Hey, I haven't lived for 50 years and learned nothing, even if I have been blinded by all the light coming from this birthday cake!)

O.K. All together now: "*Happy Birthday to yoooouuu, Happy Birthday to meeeeee, Yes we'll gather at the riiiivvverrr, the beautiful, the beautiful riiiiiiverrrrr...*"

Just wait for the light to shine through
By MaryLee Marilee © 2000

Every life has its measure of pleasure and pain,
It takes laughter and tears, like the sun and the rain,
For the flowers of courage to blossom anew,
If you wait for the light to shine through.

When the mountains of worry and anger arise
And the boulders of sorrow bring heartache and sighs
Take the chisel of love faith has given to you,
And work, so the light can shine through.

In the valley of trouble we struggle and cry;
And the more that we stumble, the harder we try.
When you come to the bottom of all you can do
Look up, for the light to shine through.

Though a tempest swells round you with heartache and fear,
Taking all you possess, every one you hold dear,
Forge ahead on the path life has opened to you
While you wait for the light to shine through.

For in every "good-bye" there's another "hello,"
And each smile holds the promise of kindness, you know.
So look forward, not back on the life you once knew,
As you wait for the light to shine through.

And the more that you laugh, the more that you play,
And the more that you give of yourself every day,
Every treasure you share finds its way back to you,
So wait for the light to shine through.

Though the tempest swells round you with heartache and fear,
Taking all you possess, every one you hold dear,
Take this message of hope to your heart, hold it true

And wait for the light to shine through…

…Just wait for the light to shine through.

About the Author:

MaryLee Marilee
(With a name like that, how can I help but spread a little sunshine!)

Think of *The Crackpot* (MaryLee Marilee) as a cheerleader for the human spirit—a light shining through the cracks of a resurrected pot that helps to keep folks moving forward, instead of wandering alone in the dark. Heaven knows, even the best of us need a little encouragement to "keep on keepin' on."

After moving 19 times, raising three kids, and living in too many homes to count (including a tipi), ML now lives full time in her 26' motorhome, traveling coast to coast visiting her eight grandchildren.

Call her a glorified "bag lady" if you will.

"In my own hair-brained way, I do my best to help folks find a smile while coping with the foul-balls life has a way of zinging at us."

Contact ML at **Maryleemarilee@gmail.com**
or **Marylee@Hearthstones.net**